OPPOSING
VIEWPOINTS®
SERIES

Breast Cancer

Other Books of Related Interest:

Opposing Viewpoints Series

Abortion
Addiction

Human Genetics

Medical Testing

Obesity

Women's Health

At Issue Series

The Affordable Care Act

Cancer

Medical Malpractice

Organic Food

Should Vaccinations Be Mandatory?

Current Controversies Series

Drug Legalization

Medical Ethics

Medicare

Prescription Drugs

"Congress shall make no law . . . abridging the freedom of speech, or of the press."

First Amendment to the US Constitution

The basic foundation of our democracy is the First Amendment guarantee of freedom of expression. The Opposing Viewpoints series is dedicated to the concept of this basic freedom and the idea that it is more important to practice it than to enshrine it.

OPPOSING
VIEWPOINTS®
SERIES

Breast Cancer

Dedria Bryfonski, Book Editor

GREENHAVEN PRESS
A part of Gale, Cengage Learning

GALE
CENGAGE Learning·

Farmington Hills, Mich • San Francisco • New York • Waterville, Maine
Meriden, Conn • Mason, Ohio • Chicago

GALE
CENGAGE Learning

Judy Galens, *Manager, Frontlist Acquisitions*

© 2016 Greenhaven Press, a part of Gale, Cengage Learning.

Gale and Greenhaven Press are registered trademarks used herein under license.

For more information, contact:
Greenhaven Press
27500 Drake Rd.
Farmington Hills, MI 48331-3535
Or you can visit our Internet site at gale.cengage.com

LIBRARY OF CONGRESS CATALOGING-IN-PUBLICATION DATA

Breast cancer / Dedria Bryfonski, book editor.
    pages cm. -- (Opposing viewpoints)
    Includes bibliographical references and index.
    ISBN 978-0-7377-7550-1 (hardcover) -- ISBN 978-0-7377-7551-8 (pbk.)
    1. Breast--Cancer--Juvenile literature. 2. Breast--Cancer--Prevention--Juvenile literature. I. Bryfonski, Dedria.
    RC280.B8B6642 2016
    616.99'449--dc23
                        2015025544

Printed in the United States of America
    1 2 3 4 5   20 19 18 17 16

Contents

Chapter 3: Does Abortion Increase the Risk of Breast Cancer?

Why Consider Opposing Viewpoints?

> "The only way in which a human being can make some approach to knowing the whole of a subject is by hearing what can be said about it by persons of every variety of opinion and studying all modes in which it can be looked at by every character of mind. No wise man ever acquired his wisdom in any mode but this."
>
> *John Stuart Mill*

In our media-intensive culture it is not difficult to find differing opinions. Thousands of newspapers and magazines and dozens of radio and television talk shows resound with differing points of view. The difficulty lies in deciding which opinion to agree with and which "experts" seem the most credible. The more inundated we become with differing opinions and claims, the more essential it is to hone critical reading and thinking skills to evaluate these ideas. Opposing Viewpoints books address this problem directly by presenting stimulating debates that can be used to enhance and teach these skills. The varied opinions contained in each book examine many different aspects of a single issue. While examining these conveniently edited opposing views, readers can develop critical thinking skills such as the ability to compare and contrast authors' credibility, facts, argumentation styles, use of persuasive techniques, and other stylistic tools. In short, the Opposing Viewpoints Series is an ideal way to attain the higher-level thinking and reading skills so essential in a culture of diverse and contradictory opinions.

In addition to providing a tool for critical thinking, Opposing Viewpoints books challenge readers to question their own strongly held opinions and assumptions. Most people form their opinions on the basis of upbringing, peer pressure, and personal, cultural, or professional bias. By reading carefully balanced opposing views, readers must directly confront new ideas as well as the opinions of those with whom they disagree. This is not to argue simplistically that everyone who reads opposing views will—or should—change his or her opinion. Instead, the series enhances readers' understanding of their own views by encouraging confrontation with opposing ideas. Careful examination of others' views can lead to the readers' understanding of the logical inconsistencies in their own opinions, perspective on why they hold an opinion, and the consideration of the possibility that their opinion requires further evaluation.

Evaluating Other Opinions

To ensure that this type of examination occurs, Opposing Viewpoints books present all types of opinions. Prominent spokespeople on different sides of each issue as well as well-known professionals from many disciplines challenge the reader. An additional goal of the series is to provide a forum for other, less known, or even unpopular viewpoints. The opinion of an ordinary person who has had to make the decision to cut off life support from a terminally ill relative, for example, may be just as valuable and provide just as much insight as a medical ethicist's professional opinion. The editors have two additional purposes in including these less known views. One, the editors encourage readers to respect others' opinions—even when not enhanced by professional credibility. It is only by reading or listening to and objectively evaluating others' ideas that one can determine whether they are worthy of consideration. Two, the inclusion of such viewpoints encourages the important critical thinking skill of objectively evaluating an author's credentials and bias. This evaluation will illuminate an author's reasons for taking a particular stance on an issue and will aid in readers' evaluation of the author's ideas.

It is our hope that these books will give readers a deeper understanding of the issues debated and an appreciation of the complexity of even seemingly simple issues when good and honest people disagree. This awareness is particularly important in a democratic society such as ours in which people enter into public debate to determine the common good. Those with whom one disagrees should not be regarded as enemies but rather as people whose views deserve careful examination and may shed light on one's own.

Thomas Jefferson once said that "difference of opinion leads to inquiry, and inquiry to truth." Jefferson, a broadly educated man, argued that "if a nation expects to be ignorant and free . . . it expects what never was and never will be." As individuals and as a nation, it is imperative that we consider the opinions of others and examine them with skill and discernment. The Opposing Viewpoints series is intended to help readers achieve this goal.

David L. Bender and Bruno Leone,
Founders

Introduction

"Breast cancer is the second leading cause of cancer death in women, exceeded only by lung cancer. The chance that breast cancer will be responsible for a woman's death is about 1 in 36 (about 3%). Death rates from breast cancer have been declining since about 1989, with larger decreases in women younger than 50. These decreases are believed to be the result of earlier detection through screening and increased awareness, as well as improved treatment."

—American Cancer Society,
"What Are the Key Statistics
About Breast Cancer?,"
September 25, 2014

Abigail "Nabby" Adams Smith, the daughter of John Adams, the second president of the United States, and his wife, Abigail, was diagnosed in 1810 with breast cancer at the age of forty-five. The first treatment prescribed by her Boston physician was hemlock pills, to "poison the disease." That treatment proved ineffective, and John and Abigail explored other options for their daughter. In October 1811, a mastectomy was performed on Smith without any anesthesia. Although the breast was removed, cancer cells remained and spread to other parts of Smith's body. She died of breast cancer in August 1813.

Mastectomy—performed more humanely—still remains a major weapon in the battle against breast cancer. Former first ladies Betty Ford and Nancy Reagan were both diagnosed with breast cancer while their husbands were presidents. Ford underwent a mastectomy followed by chemotherapy. Reagan, whose cancer was caught at an earlier stage, had a mastectomy without radiation or chemotherapy. Both women are considered long-term survivors of breast cancer.

Although the war on breast cancer is far from over, significant progress has been made. It is no longer a death sentence, as it was considered in the 1810s. The prognosis for women diagnosed in the twenty-first century is improved over that in the 1970s and 1980s, when Ford and Reagan were diagnosed, respectively. Early detection and advances in surgery, drug therapies, and radiation therapy have caused the mortality rate from breast cancer to fall by more than a third since the 1980s. Nine out of ten women with breast cancer are alive five years after their diagnoses, according to the American Society of Clinical Oncology.

While fewer women are dying from breast cancer, more are being diagnosed with it. A woman in the United States has a one in eight chance of developing breast cancer in her lifetime, contrasted to a one in eleven risk in the 1970s. According to the American Cancer Society, the increased risk is due to women living longer; changes in reproductive patterns, including having fewer children and having them later in life; menopausal hormone use; and increased detection from screening.

Breast cancer occurs when there are abnormal changes to the genes in breast cells that cause those cells to multiply without control, forming a tumor. About 80 percent of breast cancers are ductal carcinomas, which are cancers that originate in the milk ducts of the breast. About 10 percent of breast cancers are lobular carcinomas, cancers that begin in the milk-producing glands. There are other, less common breast cancers, including cancer beginning in the stromal tissues. Breast cancer confined to the breast is not fatal; death occurs when the cancer metastasizes, or spreads to other parts of the body. Cancer cells can be carried throughout the body in either the bloodstream or lymphatic system. These abnormal cells multiply in their new setting, growing into new tumors. The most common places breast cancer spreads are the bones, liver, and lungs.

Ancient Egyptians are generally credited with being the first to recognize breast cancer as a disease more than three thousand years ago. Hippocrates, considered the father of Western medicine, described breast cancer as a humoral disease:

> For Hippocrates, the body consisted of four "humors" (blood, phlegm, yellow bile, and black bile), which mirrored the building blocks of nature (air, fire, earth, and water)— and an imbalance of the system of humors caused sickness or even death. For Hippocrates, cancer was caused by the excess of black bile, or "melonchole." This logic made sense to Hippocrates because the appearance of an untreated breast tumor would be black and hard, eventually erupting through the skin with black fluids.

Physicians in the eighteenth century gradually concluded that breast cancer was a localized disease and looked to surgery as a cure. French physicians Henri Le Dran and Claude-Nicolas Le Cat argued that breast tumors could be surgically removed before they spread. However, until anesthesia was introduced in 1846, surgery was a drastic option. The first radical mastectomy—with the breast, chest muscle, and lymph nodes being removed—was performed by William Stewart Halsted in 1882. Radical mastectomies became the gold standard of breast cancer treatment and were used extensively from 1895 to the mid-1970s.

In 1955, Cleveland Clinic–based surgeon George Crile Jr., following the work of Scottish surgeon Reginald Murley, among others, began advocating for more conservative breast cancer surgery. In the mid-1950s, Bernard Fisher challenged the standard practice of radical mastectomies, advocating breast-conserving surgery followed by radiation or chemotherapy to treat many breast cancers. Fisher's research led him to dispute Halsted's theory that breast cancer cells always passed through the lymph nodes before metastasizing throughout the body. Because breast cancer is a systemic disease, Fisher argued, if metastasis occurs prior to surgery, a radical mastectomy will not halt the disease. As chairman of the National Surgical Adjuvant Breast and Bowel Project (NSABBP), Fisher conducted trials over a course of three decades that demonstrated that either a total mastectomy or a lumpectomy plus radiation treatment were as effective as radical mastectomy. His trials also validated the use of tamoxifen to both treat and prevent breast cancer and the practice of administering chemotherapy prior to surgery to reduce the size of breast tumors. By 1995, fewer than 10 percent of the women diagnosed with breast cancer had a mastectomy.

In the twenty-first century, important advances have been made in the prevention and treatment of breast cancer. Because obesity is a risk factor for breast cancer, more attention has been drawn to the importance of a healthy diet and exercise to prevent cancer. Genetic testing has enabled physicians to determine the most effective treatment for patients—in particular, which patients would benefit from chemotherapy as well as hormone therapy. For the one in five breast cancer patients who test positive for the human epidermal growth factor receptor 2 (HER2), which promotes the growth of breast cancer cells, drugs that target this protein have proven effective in treating and preventing the recurrence of breast cancer.

Despite the advances that have been made in treating and detecting breast cancer, it remains the second deadliest cancer for women, behind lung cancer. In *Opposing Viewpoints: Breast Cancer*, physicians, researchers, commenters, and journalists offer varying opinions on the issues surrounding the disease in chapters titled "Do Annual Mammograms Save Lives?," "Does Preventive Mastectomy Save Lives?," "Does Abortion Increase the Risk of Breast Cancer?," and "Has Breast Cancer Awareness Become Commercialized?"

CHAPTER 1

Do Annual Mammograms Save Lives?

Chapter Preface

Having a baseline mammogram taken at age forty has become a rite of passage for American women, with 67 percent of all women over the age of forty getting a mammogram each year. Despite its ubiquity, mammography has been the subject of controversy since its introduction in the late 1950s. The controversies surrounding mammography are social and cultural, as well as scientific.

A surgeon in Berlin, Albert Salomon, was the first to use X-ray technology to detect breast cancer. Using X-ray images, he studied the breast cancer tissues removed from three thousand women who had undergone mastectomies. He was able to distinguish between cancerous and noncancerous tissue and published his findings in 1913 but did not use mammography in his medical practice.

Although X-rays were used as diagnostic tools for a variety of diseases in the first half of the twentieth century, mammography was considered an unreliable tool. Additionally, American women were uncomfortable baring their breasts to doctors, who were invariably men.

It would take until the late 1950s before significant advances were made in mammography. Considered the father of modern mammography, Robert L. Egan, a radiology resident at the MD Anderson Cancer Center, was given the challenge by the head of radiation to develop an X-ray that would accurately detect breast cancer. Egan's research was unpopular at the time. By changing the type of X-ray film and finding the optimal settings, Egan was able to get clearer images that were easier to interpret. Between 1956 and 1959, Egan and his colleagues used his technique on one thousand women who did not present with breast cancer through physical examination. Of these women, 245 were found to have breast cancer through biopsy, and Egan identified 238 of these cancers through mammography. The combination of improved technology and this impressive success rate in detecting breast cancer vindicated Egan's work, and mammography use became much more widespread.

In December 1971, President Richard Nixon signed the National Cancer Act into law, representing the nation's declaration of war on cancer. One of the programs emanating from this act was the Breast Cancer Detection Demonstration Project (BCDDP), which planned for the screening of more than 250,000 American women for breast cancer using mammography.

However, not all physicians embraced mammography. John C. Bailar of the National Cancer Institute published an article in 1976 in the *Annals of Internal Medicine* expressing concerns that routine mammography detected slow-growing malignancies unlikely to ever become lethal. Additionally, he argued that the risk that the radiation in mammograms could cause cancer was greater than the perceived benefits from mammography. Despite these cautions, in 1976 the American Cancer Society recommended mammography as a screening tool. The founding of the Susan G. Komen organization in 1982 added another influential voice to advocacy for annual mammograms. By 1987, 29 percent of American women over age forty reported having an annual mammogram, a rate that would rise to 70 percent by 2000. Improvements continued to be made to mammography technology, including digital mammograms in 2000 and 3-D technology in 2011. In 2009, the American Cancer Society announced that breast cancer rates were down 30 percent since their peak in 1991 and attributed this to improvements in early detection and treatment.

In 2009, the US Preventive Services Task Force reported that mammograms provided little benefit to women under fifty. This touched off heated debate about the benefits of mammography. In the following chapter, physicians, journalists, and commentators debate the pros and cons associated with mammography.

"It's irresponsible to say mammography doesn't lead to improved survival based on this study."

About That Study That Says Mammograms Don't Save Lives ... What You Need to Know

Robin Hilmantel

Robin Hilmantel is the deputy editor at Women's Health *magazine. In the following viewpoint, Hilmantel argues that women should not stop having annual mammograms based on the results of the study published in the* British Medical Journal (BMJ). *She claims that some critics of the study state that it was not a random trial because nurses may have put women with larger tumors in the mammogram group so that they would receive additional care that could improve their survival chances. Hilmantel concludes that because there is conflicting evidence as to the value of mammograms, women should continue to get them annually.*

As you read, consider the following questions:

1. According to Hilmantel, how many women died in the mammogram group and the control group in the Canadian National Breast Screening Study?

2. What evidence does Dr. Marisa Weiss cite to back up her claim that the Canadian study was not a random trial?

3. According to the viewpoint, what are some of the other issues that Dr. Weiss finds with the trial?

The idea behind getting a yearly mammogram starting at age 40 (or 50, depending on whose guidelines you're following) is pretty straightforward: If you can detect breast cancer earlier, you can improve your odds of survival. But a new study published in the *British Medical Journal* is questioning that logic: According to its findings, mammograms may not cut mortality risk. It adds even more intensity to a question that's been hotly debated by the medical community in recent years: Are mammograms worthwhile?

Every medical test comes with both potential risks and benefits to consider—and some experts are becoming increasingly vocal about their belief that the guidelines for who should get mammograms and how often should be revisited. While this study has certainly added fuel to the fire, it shouldn't cause you to steer clear of mammograms—here's why.

The New Findings

For the *British Medical Journal* study, Canadian researchers looked at data from the Canadian National Breast Screening Study, which recruited 89,835 women who were 40–59 at the beginning of the study, gave each of them a clinical breast exam, then assigned each participant to one of two groups: a group that would receive annual mammograms *and* clinical breast exams for the next four years, or a group that would receive only annual clinical breast exams for the next four years (or, in the case of the women 40–49, would just remain under the care of their regular doctors). Researchers then continued to follow up with the participants until 25 years after their original recruitment.

During the initial screening period, a total of 1,190 breast cancers were diagnosed (666 in the mammography group, and 524 in the control group). The tumors detected by mammograms did tend to be slightly smaller and were a little less likely to be node positive (meaning they had cancerous cells in them). But the mortality rate didn't differ much between the two groups: During the 25-year follow-up period, 180 women in the mammogram group died, compared to 171 women in the control group.

If you look at the entire study period, 3,250 women in the mammogram group and 3,133 in the control group were diagnosed with breast cancer. The number who died were, again, virtually identical: 500 women in the mammogram group, compared to 505 in the control group.

What's more, the study authors are asserting that about one in five of the breast cancer diagnoses made as a result of mammograms were overdiagnoses. In other words, had these tumors not been detected, researchers say they never would have caused health issues or required treatment.

"Early detection could be of greater benefit in communities where most cancers that present clinically are larger and a higher proportion are node positive," write the researchers (who could not be reached for comment for this article). "However, in technically advanced countries, our results support the views of some commentators that the rationale for screening by mammography should be urgently reassessed by policy makers."

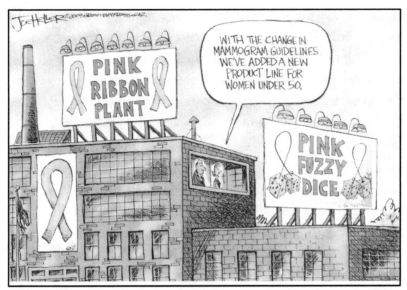

But Was It Truly a Random Trial?

While the study authors say the women were randomly placed in either the mammogram group or the control group, some members of the medical community claim that, after examining the women at the onset of the study, nurses may have put women with larger cancers into the mammogram group so they would receive better care and improve their odds of survival, says Marisa Weiss, M.D., president and founder of Breastcancer.org.

"When you look at the methods section and it says 68 percent of the cancers in the mammography arm were palpable [meaning they were big enough to be detected without a mammogram], that doesn't make sense," says Weiss, who notes that the number should be much smaller if the women were truly placed randomly into either the experimental or control group. "They were more likely to go in the mammography arm because [the nurses] wanted them to have more comprehensive care, but it also made the mammography arm look worse because it had more cancers in it."

The researchers state in the study text that the nurses played no role in assigning participants to one group or the other—that the randomization was blinded:

"The examiners had no role in the randomisation that followed; this was performed by the study coordinators in each centre. Randomisation was individual and stratified by centre and five year age group. Irrespective of the findings on physical examination, women aged 40–49 were independently and blindly assigned randomly to receive mammography or no mammography."

The American College of Radiology has openly disputed this claim and has gone as far as to state that the randomization *couldn't* have been blinded:

"To be valid, randomized, controlled trials (RCT) must employ a system to ensure that the assignment of women to the screening group or the unscreened control group is random. Nothing can/should be known about participants until they have been assigned to one of these groups. The Canadian National Breast Screening Study violated these fundamental rules. Every woman first had a clinical breast examination by a trained nurse so that they knew which women had breast lumps, many of which were cancers, and which women had large lymph nodes in their armpits, many of which indicated advanced cancer. Before assigning the women to be in the group offered screening or the control women, investigators knew who had large incurable cancers. This was a major violation of RCT protocol. It most likely resulted in the statistically significant excess of women with advanced breast cancers assigned to the screening arm compared to those assigned to the control arm. This guaranteed more deaths among the screened women than the control women."

Other Issues

Even if this new research were based on a truly randomized trial, there are still some issues with it, says Weiss. For one thing, it looks only at survival—and not at other factors like quality of life. "The fact is that there are other things that are important to women besides, 'Are you alive or dead?'" she says. "Most women would like to be diagnosed at an earlier stage when they can avoid chemotherapy." While this study didn't look at whether women were able to avoid chemotherapy or improve their quality of life in any other way by getting mammograms, it's worth noting that women in the mammography group tended to have their cancers detected when they were smaller (even with the potential contamination, which would have inflated the average tumor size in the mammogram group).

Technology has also advanced quite a bit since the data was collected for this study. "When you're talking about mammograms for women who are 40–49 who have dense breasts, we know that digital mammography is better than film screen, which is what they used in the test," says Weiss. "If you're thinking about predicting accidents on the street and you used data on car-safety standards from 25 years ago, would you ever do that? Would you ever choose to cast future guidelines based on old-fashioned technology?"

As for the issue of overdiagnoses—and the fact that study authors say one in five of the tumors detected by mammography fall into this category—Weiss says there's no one medical definition as to what that means exactly. "That's an assumption that requires a judgment that's not necessarily true," she says. "Each study has to make its own claim about what researchers think is worth finding and what isn't." In other words, one in five of the masses detected by mammograms fit the definition these study authors came up with—but not all medical professionals agree on which tumors are "worth" detecting and which ones would be harmless if they were never identified.

The Future of Mammogram Guidelines

In an ideal world, only women in certain subgroups who are at a particularly high risk of getting breast cancer would receive mammograms, says Weiss. We're moving toward that—but at this point, Weiss says that we simply don't have enough information about who's most at risk to advise the general female population against getting regular mammograms.

"Most people who get breast cancer don't have a family history, don't have a gene abnormality," says Weiss. "There's nothing about them that makes it obvious that they need a mammogram. . . . We want to get to a place where we're recommending mammograms earlier on to the women who really need it and not recommending it to the women who don't, but the default of 'just talk to your doctor and decide if you need one' I believe is irresponsible because we don't know enough to identify who has a high risk at this point."

And as the authors of this new research point out in their study, its findings contradict those of many other studies that have investigated the impact of getting regular mammograms. The fact is that there *is* conflicting evidence on the effectiveness of mammograms right now. We don't know for sure that mammograms are beneficial for every woman.

That said, the risk associated with getting a mammogram—namely, a small amount of exposure to radiation (about the same amount you'd get by getting an X-ray at your dentist's office)—is minimal. So at this point, Weiss encourages all women over the age of 40 to keep their yearly mammogram appointment. "It's irresponsible to say mammography doesn't lead to improved survival based on this study," says Weiss. "What we're talking about is the most common cancer to affect women and something that is treatable with early detection. . . . It makes sense to do what you can that's reasonable to try to find it as early as possible so that you can live as long as possible and so that you can also avoid some of the more aggressive forms of treatment, like chemotherapy."

| *"Sometimes less medicine is better medicine for longevity."*

A Controversial New Study Says Mammograms Don't Save Lives. Should We Believe It?

Jonathan Cohn

Jonathan Cohn is a senior editor at the New Republic. *In the following viewpoint, Cohn suggests that while there will never be a truly conclusive study on the effectiveness of mammograms, the study reported in the* British Medical Journal (BMJ) *found that widespread screening through mammograms led to overdiagnosis and potentially harmful treatments. It studied a large number of women—ninety thousand—over a twenty-five-year period, he reports. The study showed that mammograms had no impact on mortality from breast cancer. These results indicate that regular screening should be reserved for those in high-risk groups, Cohn concludes.*

As you read, consider the following questions:

1. What is the primary consequence of regular mammograms, according to the study from the *British Medical Journal*?

2. What does Ezekiel Emanuel mean when he says studies like this are a "Rorschach test" for researchers?

3. What are some of the reasons why there will never be a truly definitive mammogram study, according to the viewpoint?

In late 2009, a government-appointed panel of medical experts came under withering attack for suggesting that Americans were getting too many mammograms—that early screening for breast cancer, starting at age 40, wasn't doing much good and might even be doing harm. The U.S. Preventive Services Task Force, as the panel is known, recommended that routine screenings wait until women reach 50, rather than 40—incurring the wrath of everybody from breast cancer surgeons, who were convinced the recommendation was wrong, to political conservatives, who thought it was a harbinger of the sort of rationing that health care reform would bring.

On Wednesday the *British Medical Journal* published one of the largest, most rigorous studies of mammography to date. If that study is right, the experts on USPSTF deserve some kind of apology.

The study followed almost 90,000 women (that's a lot of people) over the course of 25 years (that's a long time). And it was as close to a perfectly scientific study as you'll find in this field. Researchers assigned women into two groups randomly. Women in one group got regular mammograms starting at 40. Women in the other group got only physical exams. Mammograms can pick up growths before it's possible to feel them, so it was a good test of whether detecting those small growths translates to significantly more women surviving breast cancer.

The answer, according to the researchers, is a pretty definitive "no." In fact, the researchers found, the primary consequence of such widespread screening was overdiagnosis, which led to procedures and treatments that were uncomfortable and costly and, occasionally, harmful. Aaron Carroll, the physician and blogger at *The Incidental Economist*, explains the findings:

> Of the 44,925 women in the mammogram group, 500 died of breast cancer. Of the 44,910 in the no mammogram group, 505 died of breast cancer. This was not a significant difference. There wasn't a significant difference if you looked at only older women (50–59) or younger women (40–49). There wasn't a difference if you lengthened the screening period to seven years.
>
> *Mammograms did not affect mortality at all.*
>
> However, they did affect diagnosis. During the screening period, 666 cases of cancer were diagnosed in the mammography group versus 524 in the no mammography group. This meant an excess of 143 breast cancers were diagnosed with screening. Fifteen years later, the excess settled in at 106 cases of cancer.
>
> More than 20% of the cancers detected by mammography were overdiagnosed. This means that mammography overdiagnosed one case of breast cancer for every 424 women screened with mammography. Do you know how many women we screen a year here?
>
> This study is going to make a whole lot of people upset. It's a large, well-designed randomized control trial with a really long follow-up period. The people in the mammogram groups actually complied with screening in surprisingly high

Why a Nurse Does Not Get Mammograms

Metastatic breast cancer is terrible, no question. But I agree with the writers of the commentary in the January 13, 2010, issue of the *Journal of the American Medical Association* that breast cancer is just as treatable and just as deadly regardless of screening. I've opted out of routine screening.

I might accept the statistical evidence that because I have a first-degree relative who had breast cancer, my own risk is increased, perhaps even doubled. But that fact doesn't make screening any more valuable to me than it would be to another woman—unless I believe that early detection will guarantee a better outcome for me. I don't. . . .

If there are research breakthroughs that dramatically increase the value of early detection, I'll rejoice and change my attitude toward screening accordingly.

I accept that sooner or later, I'll die of something. It could be breast cancer. It's also possible that I'll die with cancerous changes in my breast (or some other location) that never progressed enough to cause harm.

Veneta Masson,
"Why I Don't Get Mammograms,"
Health Affairs, *October 2010.*

numbers. It's hard to find fault with much of this. The data make a really good case that universal screening with mammograms does almost no good, and likely does harm.

Does this settle the question of how frequently women should get mammograms? No—because "settling" the question is simply not possible.

As Ezekiel Emanuel, the oncologist and former Obama administration advisor, explained to the *New Republic,* studies like this are a "Rorschach test" for researchers. While people who tend to be skeptical of medical intervention will see evidence that we screen too much, people who tend err on the side of early, aggressive action will find flaws with the study. Among other things, they will point out, the study is based on screenings that took place 25 years ago—when the technology itself was less sophisticated.

"There will never be a truly definitive mammogram study," says Emanuel, who was longtime head of the National Institutes of Health Bioethics Department and is now a vice provost at the University of Pennsylvania. "You're in this circle where you will never resolve the issue. You need a long timeline to get the best results, but in that time span the technology always improves—and people will always say, well, this is based on old technology so it's not so relevant anymore."

One expert has already criticized the new study on similar grounds. And among those convinced regular, early mammograms still make sense is Richard C. Wender, chief of cancer control for the American Cancer Society. He told Gina Kolata of the *New York Times* that "combined data from clinical trials of mammography showed it reduces the death rate from breast cancer by at least 15 percent for women in their 40s and by at least 20 percent for older women."

But that's based on earlier studies with flaws of their own. Emanuel called the new study a "big deal"—in part because it comes at a time when everybody from policy makers to physicians to patients is becoming more aware that aggressive medical action can have drawbacks. "We are in this pendulum swing, when we are realizing these early interventions are not all that they were cracked up to be—and that's probably true. . . . The other thing we're learning is that there are lots of cancers that are indolent. It's not just prostate cancer. There was a recent article showing that even in lung cancer we can see there are cancers that never develop into tumors that threaten people's lives."

One other thing to keep in mind, Emanuel notes, is that false positives lead to extra biopsies, which carry medical risks of their own. "This is a point I think nobody recognizes. Every time you go in for a biopsy and remove one of these nodules, you actually increase a woman's chance of getting breast cancer—you're stimulating an immune response, stimulating growth, as part of the healing process. You can have these incipient cancer cells that would have been knocked off by the immune system—you have them now growing. That's increased risk."

Mammography rates in the U.S. are among the highest in the world, thanks in part to effective lobbying from women's groups, public health advocates, the medical establishment, and the manufacturers of screening devices. But in other countries, including some with similarly high screening rates, skepticism of mammography's benefits have led experts to call for less testing—and, in one country, to eventually end universal screening altogether. As Kolata reports in the *Times*, "In a recent report, the Swiss Medical Board, an expert panel established by regional ministers of public health, advised that no new mammography programs be started in that country and that those in existence have a limited, though unspecified, duration. Ten of 26 Swiss cantons, or districts, have regular mammography screening programs."

Emanuel thinks the Swiss may be taking things too far. But this study, he says, reaffirms the growing consensus that the strong push to screen everybody regularly—not just high-risk patients, and not just at later ages—is misguided. "I don't think advocating for it is unreasonable," he says, "but there needs to be an asterisk there, a little subtlety. . . . Sometimes less medicine is better medicine for longevity."

> "The good obtained from having a screening mammogram far exceeds the risk you might have from the radiation received from the low-dose mammogram."

The Risk of Breast Cancer from Radiation Is Slight

Kathleen Doheny

Kathleen Doheny is a reporter for HealthDay, a health news website. In the following viewpoint, Doheny reports on a study from Radiology *that tracks the risk of developing breast cancer from the radiation in mammograms. According to Doheny, the study concluded that the lives saved through mammographic screening are greater than those lost to cancers caused by the radiation.*

As you read, consider the following questions:

1. How many breast cancers and how many breast cancer deaths attributable to radiation would there be per one hundred thousand women getting annual mammograms, according to the study?

2. According to Doheny, what is the lifetime risk of breast cancer?

3. According to Doheny, how many woman-years would be lost by mammogram radiation? How many would be saved by earlier detection?

The potential cancer risk that radiation from mammograms might cause is slight compared to the benefits of lives saved from early detection, new Canadian research says.

The study is published online and will appear in the January 2011 print issue of *Radiology*.

This risk of radiation-induced breast cancers "is mentioned periodically by women and people who are critiquing screening [and how often it should be done and in whom]," said study author Dr. Martin J. Yaffe, a senior scientist in imaging research at Sunnybrook Health Sciences Centre and a professor in the departments of medical biophysics and medical imaging at the University of Toronto.

The Benefits Outweigh the Risks

"This study says that the good obtained from having a screening mammogram far exceeds the risk you might have from the radiation received from the low-dose mammogram," said Dr. Arnold J. Rotter, chief of the computed tomography section and a clinical professor of radiology at the City of Hope Comprehensive Cancer Center, in Duarte, Calif.

Yaffe and his colleague, Dr. James G. Mainprize, developed a mathematical model to estimate the risk of radiation-induced breast cancer following exposure to radiation from mammograms, and then estimated the number of breast cancers, fatal breast cancers and years of life lost attributable to the mammography's screening radiation.

They plugged into the model a typical radiation dose for digital mammography, 3.7 milligrays (mGy), and applied it to

Benefits of Mammography Outweigh Risks

The predicted risk of radiation-induced breast cancer from mammographic screening is low in terms of the number of cancers induced, the number of potential deaths, and the number of woman-years of life lost. For women 40 years of age and older, the expected benefit of reduction in premature mortality afforded by routine mammographic screening in terms of either lives saved or woman-years of life saved greatly exceeds this risk.

Martin J. Yaffe and James G. Mainprize,
"Risk of Radiation-Induced Breast Cancer from
Mammographic Screening," Radiology, *January 2011.*

100,000 hypothetical women, screened annually between the ages of 40 and 55 and then every other year between the ages of 56 and 74.

They calculated what the risk would be from the radiation over time and took into account other causes of death. "We used an absolute risk model," Yaffe said. That is, it computes "if a certain number of people get a certain amount of radiation, down the road a certain number of cancers will be caused."

That absolute risk model, Yaffe said, is more stable when applied to various populations than relative risk models, which says a person's risk is a certain percent higher compared to, in this case, those who don't get mammograms.

What they found: If 100,000 women got annual mammograms from ages 40 to 55 and then got mammograms every other year until age 74, 86 breast cancers and 11 deaths would be attributable to the mammography radiation.

Put another way, Yaffe said: "Your chances are one in 1,000 of developing a breast cancer from the radiation. Your chances of dying are one in 10,000."

But the lifetime risk of breast cancer is estimated at about one in eight or nine, he added.

Due to the mammogram radiation, the model concluded that 136 woman-years—that's defined as 136 women who died a year earlier than their life expectancy or 13 women who died 10 years earlier than their life expectancy—would be lost due to radiation-induced exposure. But 10,670 woman-years would be saved by earlier detection.

The data to estimate deaths from radiation exposure was gathered from other sources, such as from patients who received radiation from the nuclear weapons used in Japan. "We really don't have any direct evidence that any woman has ever died because of radiation received during the mammogram," Yaffe said.

"I'm not minimizing the concern of radiation," Rotter said. "Everything is a balance." For example, younger breasts, particularly those of women aged 40 to 49, are more sensitive to radiation than breasts in older women, but the new study shows it's better to get the screening mammography than skip it.

I *"The fundamental philosophy behind 'early detection' is flawed."*

Early Detection Does Not Save Lives

Karuna Jaggar

Karuna Jaggar is the executive director of Breast Cancer Action. In the following viewpoint, Jaggar argues that the Canadian study published in the British Medical Journal (BMJ) *is one of many studies proving that the early detection of breast cancer does not save lives. In this study, women who did not receive mammograms fared as well as those who did because they practiced self-examination and had lumps checked, she notes. Jaggar contends that research focusing on better treatment and prevention is the key to reducing deaths from breast cancer, not early detection.*

As you read, consider the following questions:

1. What are the differences between screening mammography and diagnostic mammography, according to Jaggar?

2. What issues of overdiagnosis and overtreatment does Jaggar contend occurred in the one in five breast cancers found in screening in the Canadian study?

3. What are some of the issues that mammograms do not solve, according to the author?

Just say the word "mammogram" and many women instantly divide into two camps: for and against. The remaining women feel they can only throw up their hands while experts retreat to their various corners to duke it out. A recent study is once again bringing breast cancer screening to the headlines: in February, the *British Medical Journal (BMJ)* published the largest study on mammography to date. Yet, despite the fact that nearly all women after 40 are encouraged to get a screening mammogram, few women feel they understand the implications of this long-term and well-designed study and what it means for their own health care.

As the head of a national breast cancer watchdog organization known for translating the science from a patient-centered perspective, I know how important it is for women to have access to the science in order to make their own health decisions. For decades we've all been told that "early detection is your best protection." Yet the Canadian study adds to an already compelling body of evidence that early detection of breast cancer does not save women's lives.

National headlines often refer to the "mammography debate." Yet mammography refers to a particular imaging technology and the real issue is the specific use of this tool to screen the general population for early signs of breast cancer. "Screening mammography," to look for early-stage disease in women without symptoms, is distinctly different from "diagnostic mammography," which uses mammography imaging to help diagnose suspicious lumps that have been found by a woman or her health care provider.

The rationale behind screening the general population is that by identifying and treating cancer early, even before it can be felt, treatments will be more effective and easier to bear. For many people this idea makes intuitive sense: surely the earlier something is caught, the better.

Yet the latest study in the *BMJ* adds to the evidence from a number of studies finding little benefit to routinely screening healthy middle-aged women at average risk of breast cancer. Furthermore, these same studies have found there are significant harms to aggressively screening the general population for cancer.

The recent Canadian study, involving 90,000 women followed over 25 years in a randomized trial, found that efforts to find breast cancers before they could be felt as a lump in the breast, using screening mammography, did not lead to lower death rates for average-risk women in their 40s and 50s. At the same time, around one in five of the cancers that were found through screening would *not* have required treatment were it not for the mammogram: resulting in overdiagnosis and overtreatment as these women underwent surgery, radiation, and chemotherapy to treat non-life-threatening cancers.

Breast cancer is an extremely complex disease. Some breast cancers will never become life threatening, even without treatment. And many others will metastasize, sometimes many years out, even when caught early. Some cancers are so aggressive that current treatments are ineffective, no matter how early the cancer is detected. Mammograms can't tell us which breast cancers need treating nor can they overcome the shortcomings of our current treatments. At the same time, modern advances in systemic therapies mean that finding cancers early has become less important than when local control through surgery and radiation were the primary tools.

This conclusion demands a radical rethinking of the tenets of the breast cancer awareness movement. Mammograms don't solve the fact that around 30 percent of women who are diagnosed with breast cancer will develop metastatic disease, often after the mythical five-year mark, and die from breast cancer. Mammograms don't solve the fact that there is a steep rise in late-stage breast cancers among young women, age 25–40—for whom no medical group is suggesting routine screening mammography. Mammograms don't solve questions about who is at average, and who is at increased, risk. And mammograms don't solve the fact that black women are 40 percent more likely to die of their breast cancers than white women.

The fundamental philosophy behind "early detection" is flawed. Let's look again at what the Canadian study reveals: In addition to challenging the basic tenet of mammography screening (that it saves lives), the study is also instructive about the importance of universal access to high-quality health care. Women in the study who did not get mammograms fared as well as women who participated in screening, because these Canadian women knew to get lumps checked and had access to the medical care necessary for both diagnosis and treatment.

For 30 years the mainstream breast cancer movement has told us that early detection is the solution to the breast cancer crisis. No screening tool can prevent breast cancer. Mammography finds more breast cancers than require treating. Without saving lives. The evidence is in. We will never address and end the breast cancer epidemic through mammography screening. The problem is not simply the tool, but the basic premise.

Too many women continue to be diagnosed with and die from breast cancer. Instead of arguing about frequency of mammograms or putting hopes on another imaging tool, we need to refocus our attention and abandon the false promise of early detection.

We need better treatments, and we need true prevention.

Periodical and Internet Sources Bibliography

The following articles have been selected to supplement the diverse views presented in this chapter.

Andrew Coldman et al.	"Pan-Canadian Study of Mammography Screening and Mortality from Breast Cancer," *Journal of the National Cancer Institute*, October 1, 2014.
Samantha Golkin	"A Good Defense Is the Best Offense: How Early Detection Saves Lives," *Huffington Post*, October 28, 2014.
Janis Graham	"Do You Really Need a Mammogram?," *Good Housekeeping*, February 2014.
Beth Fand Incollingo	"Canadian Breast Screening Study Reignites Controversy over Mammograms," OncLive, March 7, 2014.
Cynthia Keen	"The Beleaguered Mammogram: Controversy, Damage Control, and Shortcomings," *Radiology Business*, April 23, 2014.
Daniel B. Kopans	"Mammograms Save Lives," *Wall Street Journal*, May 22, 2014.
Monte Morin	"Mammogram Screenings Don't Reduce Cancer Death Rates, Study Finds," *Los Angeles Times*, February 11, 2014.
Handel Reynolds	"In Mammogram Debate, Politics Trounces Science," Bloomberg View, July 31, 2012.
Stacy Simon	"Mammogram Controversy 'Artificial,' Study Says," American Cancer Society, December 11, 2013.
Liz Szabo	"3-D Mammograms Find More Cancers, but Do They Save Lives?," *USA Today*, June 25, 2014.

OPPOSING
VIEWPOINTS®
SERIES

CHAPTER 2

Does Preventive Mastectomy Save Lives?

Chapter Preface

First Lady Betty Ford's decision in 1974 to go public about her breast cancer and mastectomy was motivated by her desire to raise awareness of breast cancer and encourage women to get mammograms. Her candor was unusual for the time—a diagnosis of breast cancer was not a topic many women in the public eye were comfortable discussing. "The fact that I was the wife of the president put it in headlines and brought before the public this particular experience I was going through. It made a lot of women realize that it could happen to them. I'm sure I've saved at least one person— maybe more," Ford told *Time* magazine in November 1974. Her announcement had exactly the impact she had hoped it would. In what became known as the "Betty Ford blip," thousands of women, including Happy Rockefeller, the wife of US vice president Nelson Rockefeller, were diagnosed with breast cancer after undergoing screening.

Betty Ford is generally credited as being one of the first celebrities to speak openly about a medical condition and to draw public attention to the disease. Other famous celebrities raising awareness for diseases have included Mary Tyler Moore for diabetes, Christopher Reeve for spinal cord injuries, and Michael J. Fox for Parkinson's disease. When Katie Couric, whose husband died of colon cancer at age forty-two, had a colonoscopy on television, the number of people undergoing colonoscopies spiked by 22 percent.

In an op-ed in the *New York Times* on May 14, 2013, actress Angelina Jolie announced that she elected to have a preventive double mastectomy after learning that her genetic makeup gave her an 87 percent risk of breast cancer. Like Betty Ford, Jolie made her medical history public in a desire to encourage other women to take action.

As in the case of Ford's announcement, Jolie's had such a substantial impact that the surge in requests for genetic testing became known as the "Angelina Jolie effect." The journal *Breast Cancer Research* surveyed more than thirty breast cancer clinics and ten genetics centers in the United Kingdom in the two months following Jolie's op-ed piece. They learned that demand for BRCA1 and BRCA2 testing almost doubled during that time and remained at that level through October 2013. According to the researchers,

> Angelina Jolie stating she has a BRCA1 mutation and going on to have a RRM [risk-reducing mastectomy] is likely to have had a bigger impact than other celebrity announcements possibly due to her glamorous image and relationship to Brad Pitt. This may have lessened patients' fears about a loss of sexual identity post preventative surgery and encouraged those who had not previously engaged with health services to consider genetic testing.

According to Dr. Julie Gralow, a breast cancer oncologist at Seattle Cancer Care Alliance, "Overall, I think the 'Angelina effect' continues to be very positive. It initiated national—and worldwide—dialogue about the inherited risk of breast and ovarian cancer and it also helped reduce the stigma in women who undergo mastectomy."

Other doctors are less enthusiastic about the effect Jolie has had. According to Kala Visvanathan, director of clinical cancer genetics and prevention service at the Johns Hopkins Sidney Kimmel Comprehensive Cancer Center,

> Awareness and knowledge is always good, but the message isn't that everyone should get tested. The gene only explains a small percentage of breast cancers. As more testing becomes available, we worry that women will get tested without seeing a genetic counselor first, who is so critical in helping you interpret both positive and negative results. A double mastectomy is a reasonable thing to do in some situations, but it's not the only option.

In the chapter that follows, medical professionals, journalists, and commentators weigh in on the benefits and risks associated with preventive mastectomy.

"*Patients with unilateral, nonmetastatic breast cancer who underwent contra-lateral prophylactic mastectomy had a lower risk of death relative to patients who had single mastectomy alone.*"

Double Mastectomy Improves Survival Rates over Single Mastectomy

Shalmali Pal

Shalmali Pal is a Tucson-based writer and editor. In the follow-ing viewpoint, Pal reports that a study of patients from the Sur-veillance, Epidemiology, and End Results (SEER) database showed that those undergoing a prophylactic double mastectomy had a 23 percent lower risk of death than those undergoing a single mastectomy. Despite these findings, several breast cancer specialists warned against over-interpreting the results, Pal notes.

As you read, consider the following questions:

1. According to the researchers, what are some of the fac-tors associated with an increased risk of breast cancer death?

2. What is a benefit of presenting data to a large scientific meeting, according to senior investigator Laura L. Kruper?

3. According to the viewpoint, what is the selection bias referred to when describing the increased survival rates of those undergoing contralateral prophylactic mastectomy?

Contralateral prophylactic mastectomy improved breast cancer patients' odds of overall survival by 23% compared with single mastectomy alone, according to a retrospective analysis of nearly 170,000 patients in a U.S. database, but surgical breast cancer specialists warned that the data needed to be interpreted cautiously.

Patients with unilateral, nonmetastatic breast cancer who underwent contralateral prophylactic mastectomy had a lower risk of death ... relative to patients who had single mastectomy alone, reported Rondi Kauffmann, MD, of City of Hope [Comprehensive Cancer Center] in Duarte, California, at the 2014 Society of Surgical Oncology (SSO) cancer symposium in Phoenix. . . .

Study Details

Dr. Kauffmann and colleagues conducted a retrospective, observational study of patients identified from the Surveillance, Epidemiology, and End Results [SEER] database. All subjects had newly diagnosed breast cancer and underwent mastectomy with or without contralateral prophylactic mastectomy, from 1998 to 2010. She explained that the contralateral prophylactic mastectomy rate increased from 4% at the beginning of the study in 1998 to 22% in 2010. Her group looked at survival differences for the whole study population and for those aged 50 and up.

The total cohort consisted of 169,631 patients; 141,616 had single mastectomy alone, whereas 28,015 underwent contralateral prophylactic mastectomy. The authors performed a matched, case-control analysis with patients matched based on several factors including age, race, grade, estrogen-receptor status, and nodal status, Dr. Kauffmann explained.

In terms of patient demographics, the authors reported a statistically significant difference for some patient and tumor characteristics, but the absolute differences were small, Dr. Kauffmann pointed out. For example, 81.9% of women who underwent single mastectomy alone were white vs. 82.6% in the contralateral prophylactic mastectomy group. Also, 64.7% of women in the single mastectomy–only arm had node-negative status vs. 65.5% in the contralateral prophylactic mastectomy arm.

"This led us to conclude that this statistically significant [difference] was a function of our extremely large sample size of 28,000 patients in a matched cohort, and that the differences between the two groups were so small as to not be clinically relevant. We concluded that these groups were well matched," Dr. Kauffmann said.

The group reported that increased age, larger T classification, African American race, poorly differentiated grade, positive nodal status, and receptor-negative status were associated with an increased risk of breast cancer–specific death.

Survival Data

The 3-, 5-, and 10-year overall and disease-specific survival rates were determined for patients who had contralateral prophylactic mastectomy and single mastectomy. The overall and disease-specific survival rates were higher for contralateral prophylactic mastectomy patients than for single mastectomy patients for each of the follow-up time periods, yet consistently overall survival rates were greater than disease-specific rates.

The authors then looked to see if the survival advantage persisted when excluding younger patients in whom the high-risk BRCA mutation was overrepresented. They still found a survival benefit for contralateral prophylactic mastectomy vs. single mastectomy.

Dr. Kauffmann highlighted the limitations of this retrospective research including a lack of data on the use of therapy other than surgery. Also, information on comorbidities and BRCA status could not be obtained. Finally, "despite the use of propensity score to match patients and distribute comorbidities between the two cohorts, it is likely that some residual confounding remains," she said.

"Nevertheless, these data do contribute to the existing body of literature on contralateral prophylactic mastectomy," she said.

'Potentially Harmful'

One attendee at the SSO meeting took issue with the interpretation of the differences between the two groups, especially given the large sample size.

"I think you have to be really careful with the issues of causality and association with a retrospective study with very high statistical power," warned Kimberly Van Zee, MD, of Memorial Sloan Kettering Cancer Center in New York. "You discounted the statistical significance of the imbalance between your two groups even after propensity matching. All the imbalance was in the direction of the contralateral prophylactic mastectomy group having lower risk."

Dr. Van Zee also pointed out that "the overall survival benefit is greater than the disease-free survival benefit, proving that your contralateral prophylactic mastectomy group was at lower risk of dying and were selected to be lower-risk patients."

Dr. Van Zee said the study's conclusion that contralateral prophylactic mastectomy conferred a survival advantage was "potentially harmful and [a form of] misinformation if it's based on inappropriate conclusions [from the data]. . . ."

Dr. Kauffmann conceded that "the effect of the confounders is clearly impacting the overall survival much more heavily than the disease-free survival. Certainly, this is a difficult topic because we'll never have a randomized controlled trial. Unfortunately, short of a multicenter study where we can control for comorbidities, chemotherapy, and other types of treatment other than just surgery, it is fraught with potential danger for interpreting overstrongly."

Real-World Implications

Monica Morrow, MD, of Memorial Sloan Kettering Cancer Center, also drew attention to the hazard of over-interpreting the results.

"I think the reason that we are all concerned about this is that, while you clearly understand the limitations of the data set, what gets out there in the world is simply, '[Contralateral Prophylactic Mastectomy] Improves Survival,'" she said. "So to ask the question in a slightly different way, . . . What was the incidence of contralateral breast cancer in the unilateral arm?"

In response to Dr. Kauffmann's reply that the incidence was low at 3% to 5%, Dr. Morrow pointed out "you are showing 3% to 5% survival differences, which implies that every single patient who got contralateral breast cancer died of her disease in this followed-and-screened cohort, which we know is extremely unlikely. I would just join [Dr. Van Zee] in saying that I would be exceedingly careful in over-interpreting the data."

With these cautionary words by Drs. Morrow and Van Zee, senior investigator Laura L. Kruper, MD, of City of Hope, returned to the data to perform additional analyses. "One of the benefits of being able to present one's data at a large scientific meeting is that it allows a study's results to be scrutinized before publication. We greatly appreciate the comments from both Drs. Morrow and Van Zee since they are leaders in breast cancer research and understand the complexities of population-based studies," she told the *ASCO Post*.

Further Analyses

With the additional analyses, the cases of contralateral breast cancer in the cohort were further investigated. Within the matched cohort of contralateral prophylactic mastectomy and single mastectomy patients, 2.3% of the patients developed a contralateral breast cancer, which is low. . . .

"The people who would most benefit from [contralateral prophylactic mastectomy] are those who are at high risk of developing a contralateral breast cancer. However, by prevention of [contralateral breast cancer], we would expect the disease-specific survival benefit to be greater than the overall survival benefit, and this is not what we are seeing," Dr. Kruper said.

"In our additional analyses, we demonstrated that the low rate of [contralateral breast cancer] in the cohort has little impact on the survival rates, implying that the increased survival seen with [contralateral prophylactic mastectomy] is from selection bias: Those who are healthier or lead healthier lifestyles are either choosing [contralateral prophylactic mastectomy] or are chosen to undergo [contralateral prophylactic mastectomy]. This selection bias also potentially explains why the overall survival benefit was consistently greater than the disease-specific survival benefit in our study," she concluded.

Recurrence Rates

In response to another attendee's question regarding recurrence rates, the stage at which patients presented with recurrence, and adherence to a screening schedule, Dr. Kauffmann said her group is currently analyzing the data set for that information. Regarding those analyses, Kruper et al. were subsequently able to demonstrate that the development of a contralateral breast cancer had varying effects on survival.

For those who presented with a "low stage" contralateral breast cancer (in situ to stage II), there was an improved survival benefit whereas those presenting with a "high stage" contralateral breast cancer (stage II to IV) had an increased risk of death. According to Dr. Kruper, this also demonstrates selection bias with those undergoing routine surveillance, having contralateral breast cancers detected at an earlier stage. "The improved survival is not from the [contralateral breast cancer] but from the regular health maintenance."

> *"Our breast cancer patients face an abundance of very legitimate fears related to the . . . adverse effects and toxicities of treatment for that cancer. Fortunately, we can assure them that for the majority of cases, these treatments will be effective."*

Double Mastectomy Does Not Improve Survival Rates over Single Mastectomy

Lisa Newman

Lisa Newman is a surgical oncologist, professor of surgery, and director of the Breast Care Center for the University of Michigan. In the following viewpoint, she argues that except for women with certain genetic mutations, a woman with cancer in one breast does not reduce her risk of morbidity by having a double mastectomy. She says that breast cancer physicians need to do a better job of helping patients analyze their risk factors. Newman explains that there are three facts that physicians need to communicate to patients better: that most patients with cancer in one breast do not develop cancer in the other breast, that reducing the risk of developing cancer in the second breast does not reduce the risk of the primary cancer spreading elsewhere in the body, and that even having a prophylactic mastectomy does not totally reduce the risk of a recurrence of breast cancer.

As you read, consider the following questions:

1. According to Newman, what is the risk of developing a new contralateral malignancy for the general population of breast cancer patients?

2. What are the primary factors determining survival, according to Newman?

3. According to Newman, what are some of the risk-reducing benefits that may cause a patient to opt for a bilateral mastectomy?

Dr. Sarah Hawley and her coinvestigators are to be applauded for generating insightful data regarding factors and concerns that motivate a woman to undergo contralateral prophylactic mastectomy in the setting of unilateral breast cancer.

Fear of Recurrence Is Not a Good Reason for a Preventive Mastectomy

Hawley et al. found that fear of recurrence was one of the strongest factors leading women to choose contralateral prophylactic mastectomy (CPM). This finding clearly demonstrates that we need to do a better job of explaining and defining the significance of (i) breast cancer local recurrence; (ii) breast cancer distant recurrence; and (iii) the development of a new/second primary breast cancer. Since cross-metastasis of a primary breast cancer to the contralateral breast is an extremely rare event, and since distant metastasis from the initial primary breast cancer tends to determine survival rates,

CPM by definition will influence the incidence of only the third pattern. Furthermore, since the risk of experiencing a new contralateral malignancy is less than 1% per year for the general population of breast cancer patients, only a minority of these women will actually become bilateral breast cancer patients. Fear of recurrence is therefore a totally inappropriate reason for patients to pursue CPM, and the reasonableness of CPM to reduce the risk of a contralateral new primary breast cancer is debatable.

It can be reasonably stated that prophylactic surgery by definition is never a medically indicated necessity. Furthermore, despite the fact that a personal history of breast cancer is indeed a risk factor for developing a second primary cancer in the contralateral breast, numerous studies have demonstrated equivalent survival rates for women with unilateral breast cancer, compared with those diagnosed with bilateral/ metachronous breast cancer. Survival tends to be driven by the stage and effectiveness of treatment for the first cancer. By virtue of its earlier presentation, it is likely that the initially diagnosed cancer has established itself as the faster-growing malignancy with a lead time advantage in establishing distant organ micrometastatic disease; furthermore, patients with a unilateral breast cancer diagnosis are generally undergoing diligent surveillance and a contralateral malignancy is more often detected at an early stage.

Messages to Our Patients

It is essential for those of us who manage breast cancer to clearly emphasize several messages to our newly diagnosed breast cancer patients: First, although unilateral breast cancer increases the likelihood of developing a second primary tumor, it is certainly not inevitable, and in fact, the majority of patients are not destined to develop contralateral disease. Second, reducing the risk of being diagnosed with a contralateral breast cancer does not mitigate the mortality risk associated with the first cancer. And, finally, prophylactic mastectomy is the most aggressive and effective strategy for reducing the incidence of primary breast cancer (by approximately 90%), but it does not confer complete protection, as microscopic foci of breast tissue may be left behind in the mastectomy skin flaps, along the pectoralis, or in the axilla.

The messages above are critical: Our patients must understand that the priority is to address the known cancer. In this regard, appropriately selected patients should be encouraged to strongly consider breast-conserving surgery whenever feasible, as this low-morbidity treatment is equivalent to mastectomy from the perspective of overall survival. The question of CPM is most relevant for those patients that are ineligible for breast conservation or patients unwilling to undergo lumpectomy and breast radiation.

If a mastectomy for the cancerous breast is planned, we must then address the questions that routinely arise regarding bilateral surgery. In our efforts to clarify the reality of what CPM can and cannot achieve, we must also avoid being too dogmatic and paternalistic with our patients. There are clearly specific scenarios, as delineated in Dr. Hawley's work, where the risk of a second primary breast cancer is likely to be considered excessive by most women, and where the decision to pursue CPM may be easier. Examples of such cases would be women known to harbor BRCA mutations or women with suspected hereditary susceptibility based on a strong family history of breast and/or ovarian cancer. The risk of a new contralateral breast cancer can be in the range of 4%–5% per year in cases of hereditary disease, compared with the general population of women with sporadic breast cancer, where the risk ranges from 0.25% to 1% per year.

Conveying an Understanding of Risk

Patients must understand that the risk to the contralateral breast is predominantly expressed in the future—the likeli-

It Is Rare for Cancer to Spread to the Other Breast

It is extremely rare for a tumor on one side to spread to the other. Cancer doesn't just leap from breast to breast. In any case, cancer confined to the breast is not deadly. The disease becomes lethal only if it metastasizes, spreading to the bones or other organs. . . .

There's some indication that patients understand that, yet choose CPM [contralateral prophylactic mastectomy] anyway. The majority of the young women in the Dana-Farber [Cancer Institute] survey knew the procedure wouldn't prolong life; even so, they cited enhanced survival as the reason they had undergone it.

Peggy Orenstein,
"The Wrong Approach to Breast Cancer,"
New York Times, *July 26, 2014.*

hood of having a clinically occult, incidentally detected cancer identified in the contralateral mastectomy specimen is only 6%, as demonstrated most recently by [Tari A. King et al. in "Occult Malignancy in Patients Undergoing Contralateral Prophylactic Mastectomy," *Annals of Surgery*, July 2011], and with ductal carcinoma in situ accounting for the high majority of these lesions.

Defining the threshold for the amount of risk that an individual woman finds to be acceptable, however, can be a very difficult and personal decision. Even after a patient comes to understand that CPM is unlikely to provide a survival advantage, she may continue to request bilateral surgery purely for the risk-reducing benefits, and out of a desire to minimize her chances of having to repeat the breast cancer diagnosis and treatment experience. In some cases, this choice will be influenced by reconstruction factors. A woman may be motivated to pursue bilateral surgery if she has an adequate volume of abdominal tissue because of the fact that the autogenous TRAM (transverse rectus abdominis myocutaneous) flap can be harvested only once. In other cases the decision is influenced by body habitus, for example, a woman with large pendulous breasts who is not interested in breast reconstruction may decide that she is more comfortable with a symmetrically flat chest wall in order to avoid chest wall imbalance and the inconvenience of finding/wearing a prosthesis that matches the remaining breast.

As breast cancer surgeons, we should openly discuss these issues with our patients and present viable alternatives when feasible, such as reduction mammoplasty for the large-breasted patient. Ultimately, however, the patient must decide the surgical approach that provides her with the optimal sense of treatment satisfaction, quality of life, and comfort.

Discussion Strategies

In my own practice, I have found two discussion strategies to be particularly useful in guiding patients through the decision about CPM.

The first approach is relevant for women who are lumpectomy candidates, but who express a "reflex" interest in bilateral mastectomy while they are still in the emotional fog of processing the new cancer diagnosis. For these women, it is obviously important to stress the survival equivalence of mastectomy and breast-conserving surgery, and this is also a great opportunity to educate patients about the potential axillary surgery advantages of breast conservation. The American College of Surgeons Oncology Group Z11 trial has provided strong evidence supporting the safety of avoiding an axillary lymph node dissection (ALND) in women with sentinel lymph node (SLN) metastatic disease if the primary breast cancer is managed by lumpectomy and breast radiation.

At this point in time, we do not have comparably strong data to justify avoiding the ALND in the setting of mastectomy patients with SLN metastatic disease. The mastectomy patient with SLN metastasis is usually committed to undergo the completion axillary lymph node dissection specifically so that definitive decisions can be made regarding the need for post-mastectomy radiation, and many of these patients become ineligible for immediate reconstruction because of this possible radiation. I therefore accentuate the advantage of at least initiating treatment with lumpectomy and sentinel lymph node biopsy. The patient preserves all of her surgical options with the benefit of having more staging information. If she is found to have SLN metastatic disease then she is in a better position to avoid the ALND with lumpectomy and radiation, and the option of future mastectomy and immediate reconstruction would still be available to her in the future (after completing all of her cancer treatment and healing from her radiation); if the SLN is negative, she can either continue with the breast-conservation treatment plan or she can pursue mastectomy (with or without immediate breast reconstruction, since prophylactic mammillary radiation therapy is not likely to be indicated for node-negative disease).

The second approach is relevant to the patient requiring mastectomy but for whom delayed reconstruction is planned because of medical issues or anticipated post-mastectomy radiation. I encourage these patients to at least consider deferring the decision for the CPM until they return for the delayed reconstruction of the cancerous mastectomy, because at that time they can undergo the prophylactic mastectomy with the cosmetic advantages of immediate reconstruction.

Cost Considerations

From the public health and population-based breast cancer burden perspectives as well as for individual patients, there are additional issues to be factored into the CPM discussion. It is a basic reality that cost is relevant when it comes to sorting out the net benefit of particular medical interventions, especially those that are prophylactic. Interestingly, a cost analysis study by [Benjamin] Zendejas et al. [in "Cost-Effectiveness of Contralateral Prophylactic Mastectomy Versus Routine Surveillance in Patients with Unilateral Breast Cancer," *Journal of Clinical Oncology*, August 1, 2011] from the Mayo Clinic demonstrated that CPM is actually cost effective, compared with surveillance for patients diagnosed when they are younger than 70 years of age.

The Women's Health and Cancer Rights Act was implemented in 1999, mandating insurance coverage for breast reconstruction after mastectomy performed for cancer. This legislation promoted more widespread acceptance (and reimbursement) for contralateral mastectomy/reconstruction, but patients should nonetheless be proactive about confirming that their individual policy will indeed cover the expenses of prophylactic surgery. Furthermore, we must continue to monitor outcomes in women who choose to undergo CPM, as advances in breast cancer therapies may influence the survival benefits of this surgical approach. Indeed, selected retrospective studies have recently demonstrated that patients undergoing CPM have an improved survival, compared with those focusing on unilateral breast cancer surgery. These results suggest a survival advantage associated with avoidance of a contralateral breast cancer, in contrast to the historical data alluded to above, regarding survival equivalence for patients with unilateral compared to metachronous bilateral breast cancer. As adjuvant systemic therapies for breast cancer continue to improve in effectiveness and ability to completely eliminate distant organ micrometastases, it is likely that we will continue to increase the pool of women who are essentially "cured" of the first cancer. This in turn could potentially increase the longevity threat of a second/metachronous cancer through a renewed metastatic risk. Nonetheless, data on possible survival advantages of CPM have not yet matured to the point where it can be recommended as a medically "indicated" procedure.

Our breast cancer patients face an abundance of very legitimate fears related to the morbidity and mortality risks of the actual cancer as well as the adverse effects and toxicities of treatment for that cancer. Fortunately, we can assure them that for the majority of cases these treatments will be effective and their longevity will be protected. It is therefore understandable that the desire to avoid repeating this particular life experience may be strong. We have an obligation to explain the advantages and disadvantages, as well as the alternatives to CPM, with sensitivity and patience. We must also strive to make sure that our patients do not make premature decisions without understanding the consequences. Last, but certainly not least, we are ethically bound to offer only those treatments that we feel are medically reasonable and safe as well as oncologically sound. But we must also remember that the decision to pursue treatment and the choice between the options that we offer are ultimately rights that belong to the patient.

> "I have postulated that one of the down-
> sides of breast cancer awareness is that
> there is a situation of hyperawareness.
> Women in the United States are just
> assuming they are going to get breast
> cancer."

More Women Opting for Preventive Mastectomy—But Should They Be?

Maggie Fox and JoNel Aleccia

Maggie Fox is a senior health writer for NBC News and JoNel Aleccia is a senior health reporter and editor for NBC News. In the following viewpoint, Fox and Aleccia report that Angelina Jolie's decision to go public about her preventive double mastectomy has focused greater attention on a procedure that an increasing number of women are resorting to when faced with the possibility of breast cancer in their futures. Doctors are concerned that women are making this radical choice when there are less aggressive options available to them, such as medication and careful monitoring, the reporters state. They quote breast cancer surgeon Dr. Todd Tuttle, who wonders if women are underestimating the serious nature of the procedure. Jolie, however, reports she is content with her decision, according to Fox and Aleccia.

As you read, consider the following questions:

1. By what rate have preventive mastectomies increased in recent years, according to the authors?

2. According to the viewpoint, by what percentage do tamoxifen or aromatase inhibitors reduce a woman's risk of breast cancer?

3. What percentage of women in the United States will develop breast cancer, according to Dr. Todd Tuttle?

Angelina Jolie's surprising announcement that she'd had both breasts removed to reduce her risk of getting cancer has brought renewed attention to the controversial procedure.

Rates of women who are opting for preventive mastectomies have increased by an estimated 50 percent in recent years, experts say. And surveys show they are happy with the decision.

But many doctors are puzzled because the operation doesn't carry a 100 percent guarantee, it's major surgery—and women have other options, from a once-a-day pill to careful monitoring. Women can take tamoxifen or one of several newer drugs called aromatase inhibitors and reduce their risk by as much as 50 percent.

For Jolie, the chance to prevent cancer was worth losing her breasts, she wrote in the *New York Times*.

Like many other women having the procedure, Jolie, who is 37 and a mother of six, says she did not want to live in dread of the cancer that killed her mother at age 56. "I decided to be proactive and to minimize the risk as much as I could," she wrote.

Since genetic tests for breast cancer risks have become available, the number of women choosing to be tested and then to have their breasts removed has shot up, says Dr. Todd Tuttle, chief of surgical oncology at the University of Minnesota.

Jolie said she had a mutation of the BRCA1 gene, which raises the risk of both breast and ovarian cancer. "My doctors estimated that I had an 87 percent risk of breast cancer and a 50 percent risk of ovarian cancer, although the risk is different in the case of each woman," she wrote. She says she also plans to have her ovaries removed at some point.

In Jolie's case, her decision was "absolutely indicated," said Tuttle. At 37, Jolie is young to worry about breast cancer. But studies also show that the younger a woman is when she develops breast cancer, the more aggressive the disease is.

Other genes can raise or lower the risk that BRCA1 and BRCA2 mutations confer. And these mutations are rare. The U.S. Preventive Services Task Force recommends that only women with a strong family history even think about getting a BRCA genetic test—which is only 2 percent of U.S. women.

But why are so many women opting for surgery when survival rates for breast cancer are 93 percent if it's caught at the earliest stages and 88 percent at stage 1?

"I have postulated that one of the downsides of breast cancer awareness is that there is a situation of hyperawareness. Women in the United States are just assuming they are going to get breast cancer," Tuttle says. The actual rate is about 12 percent. About 1 in 8 U.S. women will develop breast cancer, and while 230,000 women were diagnosed with breast cancer last year, just under 40,000 died of it.

Dr. Sandra Swain, president of the American Society of Clinical Oncology, agrees that women shouldn't just assume they are at high risk. But she doesn't think there's any such thing as too much awareness.

"To me, you never can be too aware," says Swain, medical director of the Washington Cancer Institute at MedStar Washington Hospital Center. "I think people speaking out like Angelina Jolie are very good. She is very thoughtful about it." Jolie got genetic counseling and got an assessment of her own personal risk. "That's a good model," Swain said.

It's hard to determine the precise number of women who are opting to have surgery for a medical condition they don't yet have. Private insurance companies have the best information, and there's not an easy way to get it and compile a database.

Tuttle's done a lot of research looking at how many women chose to have both breasts removed when cancer was found in one breast. Although the risk of developing cancer in the healthy breast is fairly low, many women choose to have both breasts removed when a tumor develops in one.

One study showed that women aged 55 and younger with a family history of breast cancer in both breasts—a high-risk group—had about a 16 percent risk of developing cancer in the second breast over the next 10 years. Older women would have an even lower risk. Yet the rates of prophylactic mastectomies among these women doubled between 1998 and 2005.

"It is pretty clear that the use of double mastectomy for women with cancer in one breast has exploded," Tuttle told NBC News.

Another way to look at rates is to study women with a form of precancer called lobular carcinoma in situ, or LCIS for short. LCIS does not always progress to cancer, but some women choose to have their breasts removed after a diagnosis, Tuttle says.

"Rates of prophylactic mastectomy for women with LCIS increased by 50 percent since the year 2000," Tuttle said. He

---

Fatal Retraction

Not all cancers are lethal—despite the fear the name evokes. Although doctors often can't tell for certain which individual tumors are destined to be deadly, a growing number of studies suggest that many found at early stages may be so slow-growing they are unlikely to be fatal. Some recent estimates of this 'overdiagnosis' rate in common cancers:

Prostate	60%
Breast	30%
Thyroid	90%
Skin	90%
Lung*	18%

*Refers only to lung cancers detected by low-dose CT scans.
Sources: American Cancer Society (Prostate); New England Journal of Medicine (Breast); The BMJ (Thyroid); Journal of the American Medical Association and Lancet Oncology (Skin); JAMA Internal Medicine (Lung*)

TAKEN FROM: Melinda Beck, "Some Cancer Experts See 'Overdiagnosis,' Question Emphasis on Early Detection," *Wall Street Journal*, September 14, 2014.

---

presented a study to the American Society of Breast Surgeons last week showing rates of women who have preventive mastectomies after LCIS went from 12 percent in 2000 to 18 percent in 2009.

Jolie's decision resonated with women like Lizzie Stark, 31, of Edison, N.J., who had a preventive double mastectomy two years ago after learning she had the BRCA1 gene. Her immediate response was empathy for the movie star—"This is a terrible decision to have to make"—and gratitude that Jolie chose to go public.

"I think it'll make it easier, the more women who come out and talk about it," said Stark.

Private insurers usually pay for both the removal and the reconstruction, including implants, if a doctor indicates the need. And the results are good if done by a good surgeon, studies show. Women usually feel good about their choice, also—surveys of women who have had double mastectomies show little regret.

But women may not realize just how serious the surgical procedure is, Tuttle says.

"I wonder if one of the reasons driving this trend is women underestimate the extent of this operation," he said. "Prophylactic mastectomy with immediate reconstruction is a big operation. It can be five to six hours," Tuttle says. "There can be complications and re-operations."

And recovery can take a "good month," he added.

"Prophylactic mastectomy is permanent and irreversible," the National Cancer Institute cautions. "This surgery causes significant loss of sensation in the breast, which can have an impact on sexuality."

Stark, who also had nipple-sparing reconstructive surgery, said she appreciated that Jolie made a point of saying that the surgery didn't diminish her sexuality.

"I did feel like I lost my femininity," Stark said. "Because it is a part of your body associated with femininity. I started wearing girlier clothes than I had before. I started wearing more makeup and plucking my eyebrows. But you don't have to lose your femininity."

Jolie explains the motivation behind her decision: control. "Life comes with many challenges. The ones that should not scare us are the ones we can take on and take control of," she writes.

> "Racial and economic inequalities are enshrined in our health care system due to increasing privatization, skyrocketing costs, barriers to access, and historical abuse by doctors and other providers."

Many Women Cannot Afford Genetic Testing for Breast Cancer

Colleen Joy McCullough

Colleen Joy McCullough is a research assistant at MDRC, a non-profit education and social policy research organization. In the following viewpoint, she asserts that despite the heightened awareness that actress Angelina Jolie's announcement of her preventive double mastectomy brought to the importance of genetic testing in the battle against breast cancer, the costs of this type of genetic technology are beyond the reach of many women. Lack of access to genetic testing is just one example of the economic and racial inequities present in the US health care system, she maintains. McCullough contends that as new and expensive technolo-

Colleen Joy McCullough, "Genetic Segregation: The Next Frontier of American Inequality?," *Women's Health Activist*, vol. 39, no. 1, January–February 2014, p. 8. Copyright © 2014 NWHN. All rights reserved. Reproduced with permission.

*gies are developed, they are increasingly reserved only for those
who can afford them, deepening the divide between the health
care haves and have-nots.*

As you read, consider the following questions:

1. According to McCullough, what are some of the barriers
   to adequate health care that women of color face?

2. What is preimplantation genetic diagnosis, and what are
   its implications, according to the viewpoint?

3. What does McCullough say is the cost of one cycle of
   preimplantation genetic diagnosis and in vitro fertilization?

In May 2013, Angelina Jolie shocked the public with her
New York Times op-ed disclosing her decision to have a preventive double mastectomy. She made the choice after receiving genetic test results that indicated she carries a mutation
on her BRCA1 gene that significantly increases the risk of
some types of breast or ovarian cancer.* Her candor about
this important medical decision sparked a flurry of interest
from the media, health care professionals, and—perhaps most
importantly—other women.

Genetic Testing Is Expensive

Jolie's experience has heightened awareness about this type of
breast cancer prevention, as well as the potential of genetic
testing. Nevertheless, her promotion of genetic testing is prob-
lematic because most women, no matter how hard we might
wish it, are not Angelina Jolie! Her op-ed only touched on the

---

* According to the National Cancer Institute: "about 12 percent of women in the general population will develop breast cancer some time during their lives. By contrast,
according to the most recent estimates, 55 to 65 percent of women who inherit a
harmful BRCA1 mutation and around 45 percent of women who inherit a harmful
BRCA2 mutation will develop breast cancer by age 70 years."

economic, emotional, and racial barriers that many women face in the quest for genetic testing and treatments, and health care access in general.

The economic barriers women face in attempting to access genetic technology provide a powerful lens through which to examine the shortfalls of the American health care system. A little scientific summary of the technology in discussion: The test Jolie received works by screening for mutations in an individual's BRCA1 and BRCA2 genes. Finding a mutation on either of these genes indicates an increased risk of breast and ovarian cancers—the risk is even higher if a woman has both the mutated genes and a family history of these cancers.

Myriad Genetics held the patent for the specific BRCA1 and BRCA2 genes until June 2013, when the U.S. Supreme Court ruled that isolated human genes cannot be patented. While it held the patent, Myriad was able to charge as much as $3,000 for the test, which was typically not covered by insurance, putting it largely out of reach for most women. (For me personally, that's two months' worth of pay . . . and I have two jobs!)

In the near future, however, it is hoped that the Supreme Court ruling and [Patient Protection and] Affordable Care Act (ACA) implementation will help expand the availability of genetic testing and research, and reduce the costs of genetic technologies. (Under the ACA, if a health care provider determines the BRCA test is appropriate for a patient, her insurer must cover both it and genetic counseling with no co-pay.)

Women of Color Are Less Likely to Be Tested

Women of color face additional barriers. Given the contentious, oppressive, and often violent interactions between women of color and the health care system, women of color have historically been distrustful of the U.S. medical establishment. It should come as no surprise, then, that a small study published in 2013 found that African American women who have higher levels of distrust about the medical system were less likely to seek genetic testing for BRCA1 and BRCA2.

These study results are incredibly alarming, as "distinct variations in the BRCA1/2 genes have been reported among African American women," which need to be further explored. Worse, African American women have higher death rates from breast cancer than any other racial/ethnic group. Even if these women have the economic resources to access new genetic medical technologies, centuries of racism, mistreatment, and abuse by the health care system may deter African American women and other people of color from seeking the tests and preventive care necessary to make the best possible decisions for their health.

Racial and economic inequalities are enshrined in our health care system due to increasing privatization, skyrocketing costs, barriers to access, and historical abuse by doctors and other providers. As expensive genetic health care technologies gain popularity, however, there is a risk that economic and racial stratification may become embedded not only in our health care system, but also in our very genetic code. If the upper class continues to take advantage of pricey new genetic technologies while the lower classes are denied access to this high-tech health care, in a few generations we could literally have genetically divided classes. The upper class would have exponentially lower rates of health problems caused by inherited genes, while the rest of us lowly peons who can't afford these tests and procedures continue to experience higher rates of health problems.

Health Care Is Stratified by Class

This may sound like a dystopian work of science fiction, but it's not entirely implausible—thanks to a procedure called "preimplantation genetic diagnosis" (PGD). Although many of us know more about genetic testing thanks to Jolie's op-ed, many people don't know about PGD, probably because most of us cannot even dream of affording or accessing it. PGD gives parents the ability to test embryos in vitro for genetic markers before implantation; it can even be used to test oocytes before fertilization! The markers looked for could be for simple things, like the sex of the child; cosmetic attributes, like eye color; or inherited diseases (or dispositions to disease), like certain types of breast and ovarian cancers, sickle-cell anemia, or Tay-Sachs and Huntington's diseases.

Parents who can afford to utilize PGD have the opportunity to select embryos for implantation that are free of certain genetic disease markers. From a public health perspective, PGD has the potential to reduce rates of disease and raise life expectancy and quality for future generations.

It's also incredibly expensive: The cost of one cycle of PGD and in vitro fertilization can run between $12,000 and $18,000, and is rarely covered by health insurance. As it stands, PGD is essentially a modern, high-tech incarnation of eugenics. And, right now, PGD regulation in the United States is virtually nonexistent. We are the only country with access to this technology that does not regulate it in some form.

As is the trend with most American health care, any positive effects from PGD are likely to be reserved solely for society's upper crusts. While it certainly deserves considerable legal regulation and ethical consideration, much of this threat could be neutralized by a more equitable and just health care system in general. New high-cost technologies like PGD will only serve to deepen the divide between the health outcomes of the rich and the working classes. As long as the American health care system bestows the best treatment to the highest bidders, we will continue to be a socially, economically, and medically segregated country. Without universal access to new medical technologies, within just a few generations, class may no longer be just a matter of economic resources, but of our very genetic code.

> *"Whatever decision you make, you're very likely to be happy with that in the long run, so listen to yourself, and make the decision that's best for you."*

Most Women Who Have a Preventive Mastectomy Are Happy with Their Choice

Rick Nauert

Rick Nauert is a senior news editor at Psych Central. In the following viewpoint, Nauert reports that a Mayo Clinic study determined that the vast majority of women who had double mastectomies believe they made the right decision. The survey also uncovered differences between those women undergoing double mastectomies who opted for reconstructive surgery and those who did not, the author notes. Nauert reports that those who did not have reconstructive surgery were more likely to be satisfied with their decision to have a double mastectomy than those undergoing reconstructive surgery.

As you read, consider the following questions:

1. After ten years, what percentage of women were satisfied with their decision to have a double mastectomy, according to Nauert?

2. According to the viewpoint, what percentage of women having reconstructive surgery had complications requiring follow-up surgery?

3. After twenty years, what percentage of women were satisfied with their decision to have a double mastectomy, according to Nauert?

A study reviewing the decision to have a healthy breast removed to reduce risk of future cancer has found that most women have no regrets.

Reconstructive Surgery Is an Individual Choice

And the choice to have or not to have reconstructive surgery seems to be an individual preference, including issues of femininity and self-esteem.

Mayo Clinic researchers surveyed hundreds of women with breast cancer who had double mastectomies between 1960 and 1993 and found that 80 percent said they would make the same choice again.

The finding was welcomed as more women with cancer in one breast are opting to have both breasts removed to reduce their risk of future cancer.

The findings are published in the journal *Annals of Surgical Oncology*.

Researchers were surprised by many of the survey findings:

- While most women were satisfied with their decision whether they followed it with breast reconstruction or not, patients who decided against reconstructive surgery were likelier to say they would choose to have both breasts removed again;

- In the reconstructive surgery group, women who needed additional operations due to complications, breast implant–related issues, or other reasons were likelier to regret their prophylactic mastectomy, though overall, most women with breast reconstructions were satisfied with their choices.

"I think what this study does is adds some literature to the hands of the people counseling patients to say, 'Whatever decision you make, you're very likely to be happy with that in the long run, so listen to yourself, and make the decision that's best for you,'" said lead author Judy Boughey, MD, a Mayo breast surgeon.

Most of those who skipped reconstruction said they felt the same about themselves and their femininity in the long run as they did before their mastectomies and would make the same choices today.

Many of those with reconstructive surgery also felt the same about themselves as they did before their mastectomies, but some reported more satisfaction with their appearance, higher self-esteem and feeling more feminine.

Mayo physicians are studying the personal consequences of contralateral prophylactic mastectomies to help future patients.

Peace of Mind Is a Major Consideration

Women with breast cancer have many decisions to make about their treatment, including the degree of surgery to have. Options include lumpectomy, followed by radiation; having one or both breasts removed; and if the choice is mastectomy, whether to have breast reconstruction.

While double mastectomy substantially reduces the risk of cancer developing in the other breast, past studies have found

Double Mastectomy Brings Peace of Mind

One thing I knew immediately was that I wanted a double mastectomy. I know some people would think me mad, but I wanted to get rid of the cancer once and for all if I possibly could.

Having both breasts removed meant I would not have to spend my life worrying about whether the cancer would recur in my left breast. Also, I felt I would get better cosmetic results if both breasts were reconstructed using implants, rather than just the one.

Lesley Gibson,
"A Breast Cancer Victim Speaks About Her Double Mastectomy,"
Daily Mail, *March 18, 2014.*

that many women who pursued it didn't actually have a high risk of cancer in their other breast.

There is mixed data on whether breast cancer patients with a double mastectomy live longer than those who do not choose that option, though most studies show they do not.

Physician advice and a desire for peace of mind tend to play key roles in mastectomy patients' decision, the Mayo researchers noted.

"When we're counseling women considering having the other breast removed, it's a very complex and multilayered discussion," Boughey said.

"Obviously the risk of developing a new cancer in that breast has to be part of that discussion, but the literature shows that the risk for the other breast is really not that high, and that from a medical standpoint we don't need to recommend that approach."

"But it's also important to note that much of what drives removal of the other breast is patient anxiety, which feeds into patient quality of life, and it is also important to consider breast symmetry from a cosmetic standpoint," she said.

In the new study, Mayo researchers surveyed 621 women who had cancer in one breast and had family histories of breast cancer and chose double mastectomies.

At two time points—roughly 10 years and 20 years after their mastectomies—they were asked about their quality of life and their satisfaction with their decision. The first questionnaire was returned by 583 women. The results:

- A decade later, 83 percent were satisfied with their decision to have double mastectomies, and 84 percent said they would make the same choice again. Roughly two-thirds had breast reconstruction, and one-third did not;

- Seventy-three percent said they would make the same decision about whether to have breast reconstruction surgery or not;

- Those who chose plastic surgery to reconstruct their breasts tended to be married and younger. Their mean age was 47, compared to 53 for those who did not have the plastic surgery;

- Eighty-five percent of those who chose breast reconstruction were married, compared to 78 percent who did not have reconstructive surgery;

- Thirty-nine percent of those who had reconstruction needed an unplanned reoperation, and those with reoperations were likelier to regret the decision to have a double mastectomy. The follow-up surgeries were needed for a variety of reasons, including post-mastectomy complications and implant-related issues;

- Ninety-two percent of the women who responded to the second questionnaire, given to them roughly 20 years after their mastectomies, said they were still satisfied with their choice.

> *"Most women acknowledge that CPM [contralateral prophylactic mastectomy] does not improve survival, but anxiety and fear of recurrence probably influence them during the decision-making process."*

Women Overestimate Their Breast Cancer Risk When Choosing Preventive Mastectomy

Dana-Farber Cancer Institute

The Dana-Farber Cancer Institute is a Boston-based center for cancer treatment and research. In the following viewpoint, the institute announces the results of a survey that found that young women with cancer in one breast often decide to have their other breast removed because they overestimate the odds that the cancer will occur in the healthy breast. The institute reports the somewhat contradictory findings that while young women opted for a double mastectomy to improve their odds of survival, most understood that the removal of both breasts has not been shown to reduce the risk of recurrence.

"Young Breast Cancer Patients Often Overestimate the Benefit of Having Second Breast Removed," Dana-Farber Cancer Institute, September 16, 2013. www.dana-farber.org. Reproduced by permission.

As you read, consider the following questions:

1. What are some of the steps that study author Shoshana Rosenberg recommends to give women with unilateral breast cancer a more realistic sense of the benefits of contralateral prophylactic mastectomy?

2. According to the viewpoint, what is the percentage of women with cancer in one breast developing cancer in the other within five years?

3. According to the viewpoint, what did survey respondents believe to be the percentage of women with cancer in one breast developing cancer in the other within five years?

Young women with breast cancer often overestimate the odds that cancer will occur in their other, healthy breast, and decide to have the healthy breast surgically removed, a survey conducted by Dana-Farber Cancer Institute investigators indicates. The survey also shows that many patients opt for the procedure—known as a contralateral prophylactic mastectomy, or CPM—despite knowing it will be unlikely to improve their chance of survival.

Women Have Unrealistic Views on the Value of Double Mastectomy

The study, published in the Sept. 17 [2013] issue of the *Annals of Internal Medicine*, shows a certain disconnect between what many patients know on an abstract, intellectual level—that CPM has little impact on survival rates for most women—and the choices they make after receiving the anxiety-inducing diagnosis of breast cancer, the authors say.

"An increasing percentage of women treated for early-stage breast cancer are choosing to have CPM," says the study's lead author, Shoshana Rosenberg, ScD, MPH, of the Susan F. Smith

Center for Women's Cancers at Dana-Farber. "The trend is particularly notable among younger women."

The survey results, explains Rosenberg, suggest that many patients are going into this decision with an unrealistic sense of the benefits of CPM, and of the risks. "Improving the communication of those risks and benefits—together with better management of anxiety surrounding diagnosis—and providing patients with the support they need to make decisions based on solid evidence—are worthwhile steps," says Rosenberg.

In the survey, researchers canvassed 123 women age 40 or younger who had undergone a bilateral mastectomy—the removal of both breasts—despite having cancer in only one breast. Respondents answered questions about their reasons for having the procedure, their knowledge of its risks and benefits, and their satisfaction with the outcome.

Almost all the women said they opted for CPM out of a desire to improve their chances of survival and prevent the cancer from spreading to other parts of the body. At the same time, however, most understood that removing both breasts does not extend survival for women who are free of an inherited genetic predisposition to breast cancer.

To explain this apparent contradiction, the authors write, "Most women acknowledge that CPM does not improve survival, but anxiety and fear of recurrence probably influence them during the decision-making process."

The survey also indicated that women who don't inherit an increased genetic risk of breast cancer tend to overestimate the chance that cancer will develop in both breasts. They estimated that 10 out of 100 women with cancer in one breast would develop cancer in the other breast within five years. The actual risk of that happening is approximately 2 to 4 percent.

By contrast, respondents who *did* have an inherited predisposition to breast cancer—as a result of a mutation in the

Fear Influences Decision

Almost all women [with breast cancer in the study] ranked a desire to improve survival or extend life and a desire to prevent metastatic disease as extremely or very important reasons for choosing [contralateral prophylactic mastectomy,] CPM. However, most women understood that bilateral mastectomy would not lead to an extension of survival. This discordance suggests some degree of cognitive dissonance: Most women acknowledge that CPM does not improve survival, but anxiety and fear of recurrence probably influence women during the decision-making process, leading them to identify their desire to extend life and prevent metastatic disease as among the most important reasons for having CPM.

Shoshana M. Rosenberg, "Perceptions, Knowledge, and Satisfaction with Contralateral Prophylactic Mastectomy Among Young Women with Breast Cancer," Annals of Internal Medicine, *September 17, 2013.*

genes BRCA1 or BRCA2, for example—more accurately perceived their risk for cancer in both breasts.

Women Underestimate Severity of Side Effects

Even as they overestimated the benefits of CPM, many of the participants underestimated the severity of some of its side effects. Many respondents said the effect of CPM on their appearance was worse than they had expected. A substantial proportion of the respondents—42 percent—reported that their sense of sexuality after CPM was worse than expected, although other studies have not found sexual problems to be prevalent.

"Our findings underscore how important it is that doctors effectively communicate the risks and benefits of CPM to women," Rosenberg says. "We need to be sure that women are making informed decisions, supported decisions, based on an accurate understanding of the pros and cons of the procedure, and in a setting where anxiety and concerns can be addressed."

Periodical and Internet Sources Bibliography

The following articles have been selected to supplement the diverse views presented in this chapter.

American College of Surgeons	"Contralateral Prophylactic Mastectomy May Not Significantly Increase Life Expectancy in Women with Early-Stage Breast Cancer," October 7, 2013.
Catherine Guthrie	"I Didn't Need a Double Mastectomy to Save My Life. Here's Why I Did It Anyway," *Slate*, July 31, 2014.
Karen Kaplan	"Unnecessary Mastectomies: Patients More Fearful than They Need to Be," *Los Angeles Times*, September 17, 2013.
Steven J. Katz and Monica Morrow	"Contralateral Prophylactic Mastectomy for Breast Cancer: Addressing Peace of Mind," *Journal of the American Medical Association*, August 28, 2013.
Sheryl Kraft	"Why I Chose to Have a Prophylactic Mastectomy," *Huffington Post*, May 15, 2013.
Bonnie Miller Rubin	"Double Mastectomy: A Pre-emptive Strike Against Breast Cancer," *Chicago Tribune*, March 10, 2013.
Elaine Schattner	"It's Not Just About Survival: Why Some Breast Cancer Patients Opt for Surgery on Both Sides," *Forbes*, July 29, 2014.
Debra Sherman	"Surgeons Worry Women Are Too Quick to Remove Their Breasts at Any Sign of Cancer," Reuters, September 25, 2013.
Sheila Weller	"The Double Standard in the Crazy Debate over Angie's New Breasts," *Washington Post*, May 18, 2013.

OPPOSING
VIEWPOINTS®
SERIES

CHAPTER 3

Does Abortion Increase the Risk of Breast Cancer?

Chapter Preface

There are a number of factors that have been proven to increase a woman's risk of breast cancer. The American Cancer Society divides these into two categories—factors not related to personal choice and lifestyle-related factors.

Many of the factors associated with breast cancer risk are linked to estrogen. According to the Cornell University Program on Breast Cancer and Environmental Risk Factors, "One characteristic of a cancer cell is that it multiplies out of control. . . . Since estrogen stimulates cell division, it can increase the chance of making a DNA copying error in a dividing breast cell."

Simply being a woman is the main risk factor in developing breast cancer, since men have less of the female hormone estrogen. The length of a woman's menstrual cycle impacts her risk of breast cancer. Women who begin their period at a younger age and enter menopause at an older age have a greater lifetime exposure to estrogen, which increases their breast cancer risk. In the same way, pregnancy and breast-feeding reduce a woman's number of menstrual cycles, and thus her exposure to estrogen, reducing her risk of breast cancer. Childless women and women who have their first child after the age of thirty have a higher risk of breast cancer than women giving birth before age thirty. Having a child before twenty years of age reduces a woman's breast cancer risk by 50 percent, compared to women with no children. The more children a woman has, the lower her risk of breast cancer. Hormone replacement therapy (HRT), which consists of estrogen, or estrogen combined with progestin, also has been conclusively shown to increase breast cancer risk. A study of one million women by Cancer Research UK determined that using HRT doubles a woman's risk of breast cancer. Similarly, the use of high-dose estrogen oral contraceptives has been shown to slightly increase a woman's breast cancer risk. Obesity is another estrogen-related risk factor for breast cancer. A study by the American Cancer Society determined that women who gained sixty or more pounds after age eighteen had double the risk of breast cancer than women who maintained their weight. Researchers concluded that the higher risk was likely caused by higher levels of estrogen, since fat tissue is the greatest source of estrogen among postmenopausal women.

About two out of three invasive breast cancers are found in women fifty-five or older. The longer a woman lives, the more opportunities there are for the genetic mutations that cause breast cancer to occur.

Approximately 5 to 10 percent of all breast cancers are genetic, most commonly an inherited mutation in the BRCA1 and BRCA2 genes. Women who have a BRCA1 mutation have an elevated breast cancer risk in the 55 to 80 percent range, and women with the BRCA2 mutation a risk of approximately 45 percent.

A personal history or family history of breast cancer also increases the likelihood of developing the disease. A woman with cancer in one breast is three to four times more likely to develop a new cancer in her other breast. Having a mother, sister, or daughter with breast cancer approximately doubles a woman's risk for the disease.

Race and ethnicity also play a role in breast cancer risk. White women are slightly more likely to develop breast cancer than are African American women, but the latter are more likely to die of the disease. Asian, Hispanic, and Native American women have a lower risk of developing and dying from breast cancer than white and African American women. Women who as children or young adults had radiation therapy to their chests have a significantly increased risk for breast cancer. The risk of developing breast cancer from chest radiation is greatest during adolescence, when breasts are in the process of developing. Women with dense breast tissue have a risk of breast cancer that is 1.2 to 2 times that of women with normal breast tissue. Additionally, certain benign breast conditions such as hyperplasia can create greater risk.

Doctors are quick to caution that having a risk factor does not mean a woman will develop breast cancer. Many women who develop breast cancer have no known risk factors, other than being female.

While organizations such as the American Cancer Society, National Cancer Institute, and Mayo Clinic are in agreement that the factors discussed above are risk factors for breast cancer, they deny any link between abortion and breast cancer. However, some experts point to studies they argue prove such a link. In the following chapter, physicians, journalists, and commentators debate the link between abortion and breast cancer.

"There is a well-known and documented physiology supporting both induced abortion and hormonal contraceptives as risk factors for breast cancer."

Abortion Increases Breast Cancer Risk

Angela Lanfranchi

Angela Lanfranchi is clinical assistant professor of surgery at Robert Wood Johnson Medical School. In the following viewpoint, Lanfranchi explains that it is a generally accepted fact that having a full-term pregnancy protects a woman against breast cancer. She goes on to argue that if the pregnancy is ended through abortion, the mother's breasts will have only partially matured. Breast cells only fully mature when lactation occurs, and this makes the cells more cancer resistant, Lanfranchi relates.

As you read, consider the following questions:

1. Why does a first trimester spontaneous abortion, or miscarriage, have no impact on breast cancer risk, according to the author?

Angela Lanfranchi, "Normal Breast Physiology: The Reasons Hormonal Contraceptives and Induced Abortion Increase Breast-Cancer Risk," *Issues in Law and Medicine*, vol. 29, no. 1, Spring 2014, pp. 135–46. Copyright © 2014 National Legal Center for the Medically Dependent & Disabled, Inc. All rights reserved. Reproduced with permission.

2. According to the viewpoint, what is meant by the "susceptibility window"?

3. According to the author, what are the four ways in which a woman undergoing an abortion increases her breast cancer risk?

Since 1957, a large number of epidemiological studies have suggested a link between induced abortion and breast cancer, with other studies indicating the lack of such an association. This author and others have reviewed this literature at length and show that proper analysis of valid studies indicates an increased risk of breast cancer following induced abortion. It is noteworthy that there is a universally accepted protective effect of full-term pregnancy in decreasing breast cancer risk, and this protective effect is abrogated by induced abortion. Although the National Cancer Institute's 2003 workshop on early reproductive events and breast cancer risk concluded that there was no association of abortion and breast cancer, this author and a workshop participant have demonstrated error and bias in that conclusion. In addition, the users of hormonal contraceptives are clearly at increased risk for breast cancer, as acknowledged by the World Health Organization. The purpose of this [viewpoint] is to review the biology which underlies these associations. After all, the goal of most epidemiologic studies is to provide association which then provides clues for discovery of the pathophysiology of disease.

In order to understand the reasons why both abortions and hormonal contraceptives cause breast cancer, one must first understand three areas: 1) normal breast development and maturation throughout a woman's life from her conception through the birth of a child, 2) the "susceptibility window" when a woman is most vulnerable to carcinogens, and 3) the carcinogenic effects of the predominant female sex steroids (estrogen and progesterone) upon the breast.

Breast Development and Maturation

In the nascent times of a woman's life before birth, two parallel ridges of tissue (the "milk ridge") form on her body about five weeks after conception. In normal embryological and fetal development, the only part of the milk ridge to remain after birth to further develop into breasts overlies the fifth ribs. Cords of ectoderm (the outer skin layer of the embryo) on this ridge burrow into the mesenchyme (the middle layer of the embryo). It is from these cords that development of the milk-producing glands and their ducts will occur in concert with the maturation of its mother's breast. More remarkably, it is the embryo, and later the fetus and placenta through the production of two hormones, hCG and hPL (human chorionic gonadotropin and human placental lactogen), who is largely responsible for the final maturation of its mother's breast into milk-producing breast lobules. With this maturation through a full-term pregnancy, a mother reduces her future breast cancer risk.

A mother's breasts enlarge very soon after conception, making sore and tender breasts one of the first signs of pregnancy. Even before the embryo (or blastocyst) implants in its mother's womb, a chemical signal, hCG, produced by the embryo causes its mother's ovaries to increase production of estrogen and progesterone in order to sustain the pregnancy. After about eleven weeks, it is the fetus and placenta and not the mother which produced most of the needed estrogen and progesterone to sustain the pregnancy. Fetal developmental abnormalities that prevent adequate production of those hormones cause miscarriage (spontaneous abortion) in the first trimester. The inadequate levels of the pregnancy hormones (estrogen, progesterone, and hCG) during an abnormal pregnancy that result in a first trimester spontaneous abortion do not suffice for stimulating breast development and leave the mother's breasts unchanged. Therefore, following a first-trimester spontaneous abortion, the mother typically has no change in breast cancer risk as her breasts were never stimulated to grow. Often a mother who spontaneously aborts (miscarries) in the first trimester will often remark that she never "felt" pregnant before she miscarried; she had no morning sickness nor sore and tender breasts that she may have experienced in prior pregnancies. Thirty-one percent of all conceptions will end in a spontaneous abortion.

Pregnancy Outcomes, Breast Structure, and Cancer Risk

Pregnancy outcomes other than a full-term birth can increase breast cancer risk. If the mother ends her normal pregnancy with an induced abortion, her breasts will have already started to enlarge and grow by increasing the numbers of Type 1 and 2 lobules that developed in her breasts during puberty, leaving her breast with more sites for cancers to initiate. Lobules are units of breast tissue comprised of a milk duct with surrounding mammary (milk) glands, which are in turn composed of individual breast cells. Each breast cell contains a nucleus—a center space that contains DNA, the coded complete blueprint of genetic information that every cell in the body contains. The source of any cancer that develops in a body is the result of a mutation or damage done to a cell's DNA, the blueprint. The damage may be the result of a chemical, such as benzopyrene in cigarette smoke; a virus, such as human papilloma virus that causes cervical cancer; or even a naturally occurring hormone such as estrogen.

There is recent literature regarding stem cells in the breast that are believed to be the site for some cancers to form. At a microscopic, pathologic level, analysis of the types of cytokeratin (a protein) that these stem cells produce reveals that breast cells do not fully mature until they undergo lactation, thereby becoming cancer resistant. In other words, they are changed through pregnancy and lactation. There is also literature which reveals the changes in gene expression (this is not a mutation), i.e., the genes which are up and down regulated (turned on and off), which occur with a full-term pregnancy. This is a molecular basis for breast cancer risk.

At a microscopic pathologic level, Type 1 lobules are the sites where about 85 percent of all breast cancers arise, named ductal cancers because they arise in the milk ducts. The cells in Type 1 lobules have greater numbers of estrogen and progesterone receptors in their cells' nuclei than Type 2 lobules. Type 2 lobules are more mature yet still are the sites where 10 to 15 percent of all breast cancers start (called lobular cancers because they arise in the milk-secreting mammary glands). The longer a mother is pregnant before the induced abortion, the greater the numbers of Type 1 and 2 lobules she will have formed, providing more cells which are at risk of developing into breast cancer cells. There will be more sites for cancers to start, following an induced abortion. There is about a 3 percent increased risk in her chance of cancer for each week of gestation before the induced abortion.

If the pregnancy is a normal, healthy one that goes to forty weeks or "full-term," there will be near complete (about 85 percent) maturation of the mother's mammary glands into Type 4 lobules. Type 4 lobules have progressed through a complete maturation process. This is why there is a known protective effect against breast cancer when a woman has a full-term pregnancy. Each successive pregnancy causes more of the mother's mammary glands to mature which further reduces her risk by 10 percent with each pregnancy. Pregnancy causes Type 1 lobules to increase the number of ductules (which become mammary glands) from an average of eleven ductules per lobule to forty-seven, becoming Type 2 lobules. Type 2 lobules mature still more fully into Type 3 lobules when there is an average of eighty ductules in each lobule. Type 3 lobules have very few estrogen/progesterone receptors and do not quickly copy their DNA, thereby decreasing the possibility of mutations and carcinogenesis. By 32 weeks these

Type 3 lobules start to produce colostrum, the first milk, thereby becoming Type 4 and resistant to cancer. Studies have been done which show exactly which genes have been turned off and on (down regulated and up regulated) through a full-term pregnancy. During this time of maternal breast maturation, in the womb at 32 weeks gestation, the solid cords of epithelial cells on the fetal chest wall become canaliculized (become hollow), thereby developing the milk ducts and glands of the newly forming breast.

The maturation process that protects a woman from breast cancer happens only because the child in her womb produces the hormones hCG and hPL which prepare the mother to breast-feed. In the first half of pregnancy, hCG stimulates estrogen and progesterone levels which cause the breast to enlarge with increased numbers of Type 1 and Type 2 lobules. In the later half, hPL, which rises three times higher than the mother's prolactin levels by the end of pregnancy, enables full differentiation to Type 4 lobules which produce colostrum.

This is why women who have had a full-term pregnancy have a lower breast cancer incidence than those who remain childless. . . .

Secondary Causes for Induced Abortion Increasing Breast Cancer Risk

In addition to the "independent effect," induced abortion may increase the mother's risk of breast cancer by another effect. Induced abortion is a recognized cause of premature birth often due to cervical incompetence, uterine infection, and scarring post-abortion. The cervix is the mouth of the uterus, and its muscle tightly holds the fetus and placenta inside during pregnancy. If the cervix is damaged during forced dilatation during an abortion, the situation becomes a vicious cycle in which induced abortion is a cause of prematurity, and prematurity more than doubles breast cancer risk if it is before 32 weeks. The greater the number of previous abortions a woman has, the higher her risk of premature births in future pregnancies. . . .

A mother who is pregnant and chooses abortion loses the protective effect she would have gained by carrying that pregnancy to term. If after an abortion of her first pregnancy a mother chooses to have a completed pregnancy, it means that she has delayed her first full-term pregnancy by a varying length of time. This delay lengthens her "susceptibility window" (as described below) which also increases her breast cancer risk. A woman who has a full-term pregnancy at eighteen years of age has a 50 percent reduction in breast cancer risk than if she waits until age 30.

The "Susceptibility Window"

During the time after puberty and before a full pregnancy, called "susceptibility window," a woman's breast has a relatively much smaller amount of breast tissue than after a pregnancy. A pregnancy of any length that has normal levels of estrogen and progesterone increases the number of breast lobules in proportion to the length of the pregnancy. This accounts for the fact that the later in pregnancy an abortion is done, the higher is the mother's risk for breast cancer, as the pregnancy has left her with more susceptible cells in which cancer could initiate. This fact makes teenagers who have second trimester abortions especially vulnerable to breast cancer. There is data that suggests that a woman who has a complete pregnancy and lactates within five years of an abortion has a lower risk of breast cancer than if a woman waits more than ten years before her first child is born. It is important for women to be aware of this fact, because many women will become pregnant again within a year of an induced abortion. If that next pregnancy is carried to term and she lactates within five years of the abortion, her risk of subsequent breast cancer will be lower.

The aforementioned facts illustrate the significance of the "susceptibility window" concerning breast development and breast cancer risk. The susceptibility window is that period following puberty, which causes the growth of immature breast tissue, and before the first full-term pregnancy that induces breast tissue maturation making it resistant to cancer. . . . The longer a woman's susceptibility window is, the greater her risk of breast cancer. . . .

Carcinogenic Effects of Estrogen

The root cause of the formation of all cancers is damage of a cell's normal DNA. A person's body is made of individual cells organized into tissues and organs that have different functions. Every cell's DNA is in the nucleus. The nucleus contains the chromosomes that are made of long, specific DNA sequences, the genes. Genes control the life and function of the cell. So even though the DNA is the same in each cell, the cells function differently because of which genes are up and down regulated (turned on and off).

In order to grow, cells must replicate their DNA so that each new cell will have a complete copy of all genes. During the process of replication, errors (mutations) may occur resulting in mutated genes. If the mutations accumulate or if a critical mutation occurs, a cancer cell may form which then goes on to uncontrolled growth. Anything that directly damages DNA, such as a virus, a chemical, or radiation, may induce cancer cells to form. Anything that stimulates a cell to replicate itself may also cause mutations and cancer cells to form because in the process of copying its DNA errors can occur, such as copying errors resulting in deletions or additions to the cell's DNA. . . .

Breast cancer that is not attributable to DNA mutations that were inherited from a parent, such as the BRCA genes, are largely due to the effects of the natural, female hormone, estrogen. . . .

Estrogen alone and its metabolites can also be directly carcinogenic. For example, a particular metabolite of estrogen, 4-hydroxy catechol estrogen quinone, can directly damage DNA, resulting in mutations. Studies have shown that breast cancer patients have higher levels of 4-hydroxy catechol estrogen quinone as well has higher levels of the most potent estrogens, such as 17-β estradiol, compared with the least potent ones, such as estriol.

These two mechanisms which promote the formation of breast cancer through estrogen exposure are the reason that hormonal contraceptives and combination hormone replacement therapy cause breast cancer....

Many Women Are Unaware of the Risks of Abortion

There is a well-known and documented physiology supporting both induced abortion and hormonal contraceptives as risk factors for breast cancer. Yet these risks are largely unknown to women seeking family planning services. Without this knowledge, women cannot make informed choices when they are faced with the choice of an induced abortion or life for their child and the use of hormonal contraceptives. By choosing abortion, a woman increases her risk in four ways: she creates in her breasts more places for cancers to start, which is the "independent effect"; she loses the protective effect that a full-term pregnancy would have afforded her; she increases the risk of premature delivery of future pregnancies; and she lengthens her susceptibility window. Contraceptives containing estrogen-progestin drugs increase breast cancer risks by causing breast cells to proliferate increasing the chance of mutations leading to cancer cells, and by acting as direct carcinogens.

This knowledge is especially important for teenagers who are most vulnerable and negatively impacted by abortion and hormonal contraceptives. At a time when their breasts are already growing under the influence of their own heightened hormonal milieu, induced abortion alters their physiology in a way that results in a much higher risk of subsequent breast cancer. A common occurrence is a teenager who hides her pregnancy until she starts showing in the second trimester. The pregnancy is not revealed to others until she starts showing in the second trimester. This circumstance quite frequently results in a late-term abortion, which is made worse in most circumstances by the addition of carcinogenic, contraceptive hormones post-abortion, elevating her risk of breast cancer even more. Knowledge of her risk factors and the benefits of carrying the pregnancy to term with subsequent birth and adoption could prevent this from occurring with great frequency.

> *"Based on the evidence, the ABC [abortion–breast cancer] link should not be one of the divisive elements circling closely to today's debate on abortion. And medical professionals certainly should not be required by law to discuss it as a valid theory."*

Faulty Science Is Used to Support Link Between Abortion and Breast Cancer

Abby Ohlheiser

Abby Ohlheiser is a general assignment reporter for the Washington Post. *In the following viewpoint, Ohlheiser examines the claim of a study on Chinese women published in the* Cancer Causes & Control *journal that links abortion to breast cancer. The study used the case-control method, which relies on self-reported results that are more likely to be misleading, according to Dr. Susan Gapstur, an epidemiologist consulted by the reporter. Ohlheiser reports that women with breast cancer are more inclined to be truthful about their reproductive histories than those without cancer, thus casting suspicion on the results of the study.*

As you read, consider the following questions:

1. What is the likeliest cause of an increased rate of breast cancer in women following the *Roe v. Wade* decision, according to the author?

2. According to the thirty-six Chinese studies mentioned in the viewpoint, how much does having an abortion increase breast cancer risk?

3. According to the viewpoint, what were the findings of the cohort studies in the Chinese group that tracked women over time instead of relying on self-reporting?

In five U.S. states, physicians are required by law to tell women seeking an abortion about a possible link between induced abortion and increased rates of breast cancer. But there's just one problem: from a standpoint of scientific consensus, that link is mainly bunk. It is, however, a persistent theory, as a round of conservative press promoting a new study on the subject demonstrates. The paper, published recently in the *Cancer Causes & Control* journal, looked at the results of 36 studies in China on what activists have nicknamed the "ABC link," concluding that women who undergo an induced abortion demonstrate a dramatically increased risk of breast cancer. *The Wire* asked an epidemiologist to look at the results, just in case the theory finally had the breakthrough it's been waiting for. (Spoiler alert: it hasn't).

Breast Cancer "Epidemic" Attributed to Abortion Legalization

First, some background: The ABC link idea first got going in the 1980s, in the wake of *Roe v. Wade*. As *Slate* tells it in an extensive look at the theory, those tentatively proposing a possible link based it on an observation: Following the Supreme Court's decision ensuring women have access to abortion, the rates of breast cancer skyrocketed. Although a few early studies seemed to indicate that there could be a link between breast cancer and abortion, further, thorough inquiries into the subject concluded that such a link stood on extremely shaky evidence.

But the idea is appealing, especially among those who viewed a perceived "epidemic" of breast cancer among young, sexually active women as a punitive result of the *Roe v. Wade* decision. In fact, as Patricia Jasen explains in a survey of the political and historical context of the ABC link research, that initial observation of an increased rate of breast cancer among American women is likely due to more sophisticated early detection methods that coincidentally gained traction during the post *Roe v. Wade* period.

This is the context of today's advocacy on the ABC theory. A handful of scientists, such as Joel Brind, a professor of biology and endocrinology at Baruch College in New York, have dedicated their careers to finding ways to prove the link. Brind worked hard to promote the recent Chinese study, claiming that the only reason the ABC link hasn't caught on is because of a vast conspiracy to suppress it. The groups working against the theory, he writes, include:

> "'mainstream' abortion advocates entrenched in universities, medical societies, breast cancer charities, journals, and especially, government agencies like the National Cancer Institute [NCI]. (In reality, the NCI is just another corrupt federal agency like the IRS [Internal Revenue Service] and the NSA [National Security Agency].)"

The recent study is not by Brind himself, but by Dr. Yubei Huang et al., whose meta-analysis of 36 Chinese studies concludes that induced abortions increase the risk of breast cancer by 44 percent. For women who have had two abortions, the study claims an increased risk of 76 percent. Those are dramatic numbers. So, what's going on?

Planned Parenthood Denies Link Between Abortion and Breast Cancer

The link between abortion and breast cancer is a theory whose principal promoters oppose abortion regardless of its safety. The theory has not been borne out by research. While Planned Parenthood [Federation of America] believes that women should have access to information about all factors that influence the risk of disease, Planned Parenthood also believes that women deserve unbiased information that is medically substantiated and untainted by a political agenda.

Planned Parenthood Federation of America,
"Myths About Abortion and Breast Cancer," March 2013.

Most Studies Use a Misleading Method

"The findings of this meta-analysis should be viewed with caution," Dr. Susan Gapstur told *The Wire* in an e-mail. Gapstur is the vice president of epidemiology at the American Cancer Society. She notes that almost all of the studies cited in Dr. Huang's analysis used something called the case-control method, which tends to produce misleading results. In the case of the abortion–breast cancer link, women with breast cancer who self-report their reproductive histories tend to do so more accurately than women who are cancer free. And in countries like China, where abortion still carries a significant stigma, that "recall bias" can be reinforced. "This 'recall bias' can make it look like breast cancer is associated with abortion when it is not," Gapstur explains. Case-control methods, it should be noted, have produced links between breast cancer and induced abortion before.

The Best Studies Found No Link

All but two of the studies included in Huang's analysis used the case-control method. The remaining two were prospective cohort studies, which track women over time, instead of relying on self-reported historical results. Those two studies, Gapstur notes, did not find a link between abortion and breast cancer. In fact, the eight studies that appear to be the most reliable of the group found no link between induced abortion and breast cancer risk. "The association only became apparent as the quality of the studies decreased," Gapstur told *The Wire*, noting that some of the included studies were not published in peer-reviewed publications. In other words, the work might not be vetted by independent professionals in the field.

The ABC Link Controversy Is Political, Not Scientific

Virtually no reputable scientific institution endorses the ABC link, because the controversy surrounding it has little to do with any room for debate in the data. Inquiries into the subject by the National Cancer Institute, the American College of Obstetricians and Gynecologists, and the Collaborative Group on Hormonal Factors in Breast Cancer based out of Oxford University in England, for instance, have found no evidence of a link between breast cancer and abortion, based on high-quality studies produced on the subject. The American Cancer Society has an explainer on the controversy, clarifying that "the scientific evidence does not support the notion that abortion of any kind raises the risk of breast cancer or any other type of cancer."

Based on the evidence, the ABC link should *not* be one of the divisive elements circling closely to today's debate on abortion. And medical professionals certainly should not be required by law to discuss it as a valid theory. There's a reason the media and the scientific community at large have ignored studies like these, and it has nothing to do with a cover-up. It's just bad evidence.

"It is indeed ironic that many of these studies reporting a significant ABC [abortion–breast cancer] link have been conducted in countries such as Iran and mainland China, whereas the Western journals have largely presented a great wall of denial."

Faulty Journalism Denies the Link Between Abortion and Breast Cancer

Joel Brind

Joel Brind is a professor of biology and endocrinology at Baruch College, City University of New York. He is the science adviser for the Coalition on Abortion/Breast Cancer and the cofounder of the Breast Cancer Prevention Institute. In the following viewpoint, Brind labels the studies in China reporting a 44 percent increase in breast cancer in women who have had an abortion a "game changer" because the data refutes the pro-choice defense against the abortion–breast cancer link. Brind claims that the establishment figures in the US medical community ignore scien-

tific evidence to further their political agenda. Brind concludes that pro-choice advocates are ignoring the very real threat of increased breast cancer risk that women undergoing abortion face.

As you read, consider the following questions:

1. According to the author, what increased risk of breast cancer did a study in India find in women who have had an abortion?

2. How does the author refute the argument that the abortion–breast cancer link first gained prominence in the years following the *Roe v. Wade* decision?

3. What is meant by "shifting reproductive trends" in China, according to the author?

Just this past week [in December 2013], *NRL News* [*National Right to Life News Today*] readers learned of a bombshell—a systematic review and meta-analysis of abortion–breast cancer studies in China, which reported a 44% overall increase in breast cancer among women who'd had any abortions.

Pro-Choice Activists Deny Abortion–Breast Cancer Link

I described it as a "game changer" for several reasons, including the size of the increase; that it confirmed an analysis of studies conducted back in 1996 by myself and colleagues; that the risk increased the more abortions a woman had; and because it dismantled the most popular pro-abortion defense against the link between abortion and breast cancer (the ABC link).

Like clockwork, the pro-abortion backlash was up online before the week was out. On Friday [December 6, 2013], Abby Ohlheiser, who often writes for Slate.com, posted a hit piece on TheWire.com.

Consulting "an epidemiologist" and relying mainly on an earlier Slate.com piece purporting to debunk the ABC link,

Ohlheiser trotted out the usual false denial arguments. Those included the "recall bias" argument which asserts that due to social stigma that is attached to having an induced abortion, healthy women are more likely to deny prior abortions in their medical history study questionnaire than are women who've developed breast cancer.

Hence, the theory goes, it would erroneously appear that breast cancer is more frequent among women who've had an abortion. I have shown in numerous articles written for *NRL News Today* why that simply is not true. Ohlheiser also maintained that the undeniable increase in breast cancer was "likely due to more sophisticated early detection methods that coincidentally gained traction during the post *Roe v. Wade* period."

Clearly, Ohlheiser's purpose was to reinforce the official "truth" that there is no ABC link. She summarily states: "Virtually no reputable scientific institution endorses the ABC link." Really?

In response, I submitted the following comment to be posted after Ohlheiser's article:

"Abortion and breast cancer: The problem isn't faulty science, rather politicized science and faulty journalism."

First off, Abby Ohlheiser—not a scientist herself—addresses the issue "from a standpoint of scientific consensus." Consensus—i.e., majority rule—is entirely a political concept. And in fact, significant scientific discoveries almost always go against the scientific consensus (which even scientists call the "prevailing dogma") of the day.

When the subject has anything to do with abortion—or more specifically, any challenge to the prevailing dogma of "safe abortion"—you can safely bet that the majority of establishment figures in universities, medical societies, voluntary organizations, and government health ministries will side with the "safe abortion" crowd. So to get to the heart of such a politically loaded scientific question, one needs to check out primary sources.

The Abortion Movement Advances Its Own Agenda at Expense of Women's Lives

It's fairly obvious to me that the deniers are more concerned about promoting their own dogmatic beliefs than they are about saving women's lives. The radical feminists believe that women need to be liberated from childbearing. . . .

They are irresponsibly advancing their own deadly agendas at the expense of science and women's lives.

Steve Mosher,
"Twelve Out of Twelve Recent Studies Show Abortion
Linked to Breast Cancer," LifeNews.com, September 22, 2014.

Western Journals Are Ignoring Evidence

If one really examines the so-called "high-quality studies" that do not show the abortion–breast cancer link (ABC link), and also the critiques I and my colleagues have published in the same, peer-reviewed journals over the years (since 1996), one can appreciate the scandalous abuse of science that has permeated the most prestigious journals in recent years. Fortunately, over the last 5 years, lots of new studies documenting the reality of the ABC link have appeared from around the world in international, open-access journals, largely from Asia. It is indeed ironic that many of these studies reporting a significant ABC link have been conducted in countries such as Iran and mainland China, whereas the Western journals have largely presented a great wall of denial.

Fortunately, some facts that undergird the reality of the ABC link are quite easily accessible. Just this year, for example, a study in India found that women who'd had any abortions were at a more than 6-fold increased risk of breast cancer (i.e., a 500% risk increase). A study from Bangladesh reported a more than 20-fold (2,000%) increased risk.

Just a couple more points need to be made here, by way of correction. Ohlheiser states that "the ABC link idea first got going in the 1980s, in the wake of *Roe v. Wade*." In fact, the first major study was a nationwide study in Japan, published in the prestigious Japanese *Journal of Cancer Research*, in 1957—long before *Roe v. Wade*. That study found about a 3-fold risk increase among women with any abortions, and it certainly had nothing to do with "more sophisticated early detection methods."

Also, it is a great disservice to belittle the term "epidemic" by setting it off in quotes as if it is not real. Five years ago, a highly prestigious team from the US and China published an NIH [National Institutes of Health]–funded study in the *Journal of the National Cancer Institute* in which they flatly concluded: "China is on the cusp of a breast cancer epidemic." Of course, these authors never mentioned the word "abortion," rather blaming "shifting reproductive trends." This is really code for China's "One Child Policy" with abortion (and not as a matter of choice) its centerpiece.

Finally, Ms. Ohlheiser can't seem to find "any room for debate in the data" on abortion and breast cancer. Nice try, to shut off debate on a real, man-made epidemic that has devastated the lives of so many women in the West, and now threatens the lives of so many millions more in Asia. Add to that the fact that the majority of abortions in Asia are of females, and one might start to reconsider just who is waging the real war on women.

As of this writing—more than 24 hours after submitting my comment, it is still "awaiting moderation."

"It is a disgrace that a more honest discourse about difficult medical topics can
be found in the People's Republic of
China than in the USA."

Pro-Choice Activists Cover Up Link Between Abortion and Breast Cancer

Mary L. Davenport

*Mary L. Davenport is the medical director of the Magnificat
Maternal Health Program and is on the board of directors of the
Breast Cancer Prevention Institute. In the following viewpoint,
she argues that the medical establishment persists in denying a
link between breast cancer and abortion and is suppressing information about the complications of abortion. Davenport goes
on to say that she and other researchers and physicians have had
their work ignored and censored for decades by members of the
pro-choice movement. The attempt to ignore the study from
China showing the link between abortion and breast cancer is
just another example of this cover-up, Davenport reports.*

As you read, consider the following questions:

1. According to Davenport, what is the breast cancer risk reported in the China study for women having two or three abortions?

2. How many abortions for every live birth are there in China, according to the author?

3. Why is Patrick Carroll's work important, according to the viewpoint?

In the US we are used to abortion advocates claiming that the risk of elective abortion is relatively trivial, and major medical organizations denying any link between abortion and breast cancer. Now a powerful new study from China published last week [November 24, 2013] by Yubei Huang and colleagues suggests otherwise. The article, a meta-analysis pooling 36 studies from 14 provinces in China, showed that abortion increased the risk of breast cancer by 44% with one abortion, and 76% and 89% with two and three abortions.

Ignoring Abortion–Breast Cancer Link Is an Ethical Breach

This new article is another example of the recent excellent scholarship on abortion in peer-reviewed journals coming out of the People's Republic [of China]. There is no bigger database than China, where there are an average of 8.2 million pregnancy terminations every year, and 40 abortions for every 100 live births. Chinese researchers and physicians are unencumbered by abortion politics, and do not cover up data showing long-term effects of induced abortion, as do their US counterparts in governmental, professional and consumer organizations.

Huang's study shows an even stronger increase than the 30% higher risk found in the 1996 meta-analysis by Joel Brind and colleagues on abortion as an independent risk factor for

113

breast cancer. The Brind meta-analysis, combining the results of 23 studies, gave a more complete view than any single study. But even though it was the most comprehensive study on the topic at the time, it was disregarded by establishment medical groups.

Brind, a professor of biology and endocrinology at Baruch College, is not unique in having experienced censorship of his findings for the past two decades, including at the notorious National Cancer Institute (NCI) workshop on early reproductive events and breast cancer in 2003. This important workshop was manipulated by its chairperson NCI epidemiologist Louise Brinton to suppress critical information on the abortion–breast cancer (ABC) link. The main speaker on abortion and breast cancer, Leslie Bernstein, who had never published on this topic, openly said, "I would never be a proponent of going around and telling them (women) that having babies is the way to reduce your risk," *even though it has been an established fact, conceded by abortion proponents that this is true.*

This workshop was designed to influence subsequent governmental policy, academic scholarship, physicians, and popular perception of the topic, and succeeded in doing so. It also influenced the individual life trajectories of many women who were led to believe, falsely, that an abortion decision would not have an impact on their future breast cancer risk. Because there is a lag time between abortion and the appearance of breast cancer, the effect of an abortion is not immediate for an individual. And abortion is only one of a number of factors influencing breast cancer risk, such as family history, use of hormones, and age at first childbirth. The majority of women who have breast cancer have never had an abortion. Nonetheless, there will be some women who develop breast cancer and die from it, impacted by the failure to inform them of the ABC link, or its dismissal by establishment medical and consumer groups such as the American College of

Chinese Study Proves Abortion–Breast Cancer Link

Chinese females historically had a lower risk of breast cancer compared to their counterparts in the USA and other Western countries. However, the incidence of breast cancer in China had increased at an alarming rate over the past two decades. . . . The marked change in breast cancer incidence was paralleled to the one-child-per-family policy, which became legal in China since the early 1980s. . . .

As one of the countries with the highest prevalence of IA [induced abortion], in China, it is particularly important to clarify the association between IA and breast cancer risk. . . .

In order to update the current evidence on IA and its effect on breast cancer among Chinese females, we performed this systematic review and meta-analysis to help resolve these uncertainties and further define the effect of IA on breast cancer. . . .

The most important implication of this study is that IA was significantly associated with an increased risk of breast cancer among Chinese females, and the risk of breast cancer increases as the number of IA increases. If IA were to be confirmed as a risk factor for breast cancer, high rates of IA in China may contribute to increasing breast cancer rates.

Yubei Huang et al.,
"A Meta-Analysis of the Association Between Induced
Abortion and Breast Cancer Risk Among Chinese Females,"
Cancer Causes & Control, *November 24, 2013.*

Obstetricians and Gynecologists and the Susan [G.] Komen foundation. This is an ethical breach of huge proportions.

The new Chinese meta-analysis not only concerns the ABC link on an individual level, but also confirms the observation of statistician Patrick Carroll, who predicted the rise in breast cancer in several European countries following legalization of abortion. Again, because of the lag time between abortion and the appearance of breast cancer, the link is not immediately apparent. Carroll's work is important because he finds that not only is induced abortion an *independent* risk factor for breast cancer (separate from such factors as late childbearing) but that it is the *best* predictive factor for forecasting a nation's future breast cancer rates. Nations such as China, with traditionally low breast cancer rates, are now seeing an increase, many years following their legalization of abortion.

Censorship Should Not Be Tolerated

Unfortunately, the ABC link is not unique in suffering a systematic cover-up by ideologically driven medical organizations intent on suppressing information about complications of abortion. Preterm birth is the leading cause of neonatal death in the USA, taking the lives of hundreds of thousands of infants annually, with a cost of 26 billion dollars. It has risen 20% in the last two decades. It causes cerebral palsy, long-term intellectual and visual handicaps, and much suffering. There are 135 studies from diverse locations worldwide that link abortion and preterm birth. The relationship is most pronounced with multiple abortions, and very premature infants born before 28 weeks gestation, the "million dollar babies" that spend months in neonatal intensive care units. Preterm birth disproportionately affects African Americans. Yet the medical community, WHO [World Health Organization], and the American College of Obstetrics and Gynecology (ACOG) have long ignored this association in their official publications and task forces to combat the problem. Another big cover-up involves the psychological consequences of abortion, especially suicide, which are inadequately acknowledged by mainstream groups because they conflict with the propaganda-driven view of abortion as a health "benefit."

This year I was personally prevented from delivering a paper at a conference at the last minute, along with two other women physicians presenting papers on abortion complications, at the MWIA (Medical Women's International Association) in Seoul, South Korea. These were academically sound presentations on maternal mortality, psychological issues, and preterm birth that had been accepted months earlier. Shelley Ross, the secretary-general of the organization, personally barged into an interview with Korean journalists to attempt to prevent us from speaking to them, almost causing a fist fight. In a press release regarding this incident, she claimed that the presentations threatened a woman's reproductive rights, and further asserted that "the evidence is overwhelming and undisputable that a woman's control over her reproductive health is linked to . . . the health of women and children." But if she is talking about abortion, it is obvious that breast cancer and suicide do *not* improve the health of women, and preterm birth and abortion obviously do not improve the health of a woman's future children or the aborted babies.

It is a disgrace that a more honest discourse about difficult medical topics can be found in the People's Republic of China than in the USA. The censorship of medical journals, prevention of conference presentations, denial of grant money and faculty promotions, and self-censorship of honest scholars in academic medicine who want to tell the truth but feel they cannot, impoverish us, and should not be tolerated.

"The promotion of flawed studies to try to prove that abortion leads to breast cancer is a political effort spearheaded by anti-choice groups and individuals who primarily use these studies to reinforce abortion stigma and frighten women."

Anti-Choice Groups Use Flawed Studies to Establish a Link Between Abortion and Breast Cancer

Joyce Arthur

Joyce Arthur is the executive director of the Abortion Rights Coalition of Canada. In the following viewpoint, she argues that although pro-life advocates are citing the results of a study from China as proof that abortion causes an increased risk of breast cancer, the study's methodology is flawed. She maintains that the problem with the study is "recall bias," which occurs when people being questioned or interviewed neglect to mention certain events that they are uncomfortable discussing. Arthur maintains that the main purpose of pro-life advocates in advancing the results of such studies is to scare women, and it is not in women's best interests.

As you read, consider the following questions:

1. In the 1996 analysis that Arthur cites, what percentage of women reported their abortions?

2. What circumstances does the author cite in her contention that young Chinese women are underreporting their abortions?

3. What are some of the possible risk factors for the rise in breast cancer in China that the author cites?

Anti-choice people are using findings from a new study out of China to jump to the unwarranted conclusion that abortion causes an increased breast cancer risk. But the study's methodology and data appear seriously flawed, with the results likely reflecting "recall bias."

Many Women Underreport Abortions

The anti-choice movement has been making a lot of noise over a new study out of China, published in the journal *Cancer Causes & Control*, that purports to show a 44 percent increase in breast cancer risk for women who have had an abortion, with the risk increasing after each subsequent abortion. The study claims this may help explain the "alarming" rise in breast cancer in China over the past 20 years, which parallels the one-child policy introduced in 1979.

But the study's methodology and data appear seriously flawed, with the results likely reflecting "recall bias." This would invalidate the study's findings. Recall bias is a common hazard in case-control studies, which use questionnaires or interviews to gather historical data from participants. Results can be skewed or inaccurate because people have a tendency to forget past events, or neglect to mention them, especially if they are uncomfortable with sharing the information with researchers. For example, underreporting occurs when people are asked about substance use, criminal offenses, family background, or school performance.

Recall bias is even more of a problem when it comes to reporting reproductive history, especially past abortions. In the United States, only 47 percent of abortions were reported in the largest and most recent fertility survey (from 2002). A 1996 analysis cited numerous studies on the topic and found that, as a likely result of abortion stigma, women reported only 20 to 80 percent of their abortions. (The wide range is due to varying interview circumstances, geographic locations, or demographic characteristics of the women.) A significant body of evidence has accumulated on abortion underreporting, going back to the early days of legal abortion in 1960s Eastern Europe, as documented by Christopher Tietze and Stanley K. Henshaw:

> The classic example is the fertility and family planning study of 1966, conducted in Hungary a decade after the legalization of abortion. In that survey, the numbers of abortions reported by the respondents for the years 1960–65 corresponded to only 50–60 percent of the number actually performed. A comparable level of underreporting was also noted in 1977.

But how does an apparent association arise between abortion and breast cancer (ABC)? In case-control studies on the topic, researchers select and divide women into two groups: women with breast cancer (the "cases") and women without the disease (the "controls"). The women in both groups will then be asked whether they've had an abortion to see if the disease might be more commonly associated with that. However, cancer patients will be strongly motivated to remember and share their full medical history in the search for answers (this is called "rumination bias"), while women acting as controls in a study have no stake in the outcome and so are less likely to mention past abortions. They would be even less likely to report several past abortions because of the increased stigma. The result is a flawed study, because it will appear that women with breast cancer had more abortions than those in the control group, when they probably didn't.

This "differential recall" is a known risk in case-control studies in general, although few studies have been done to show the effect in studies on the ABC association. A 1991 analysis in Sweden compared two studies: one that used women's abortion records from a national registry, and a case-control study that relied on women self-reporting their abortions (that were also recorded in the registry). In the end, 27.1 percent of controls underreported past abortions, compared to 20.8 percent of cases. Another study took place in the Netherlands in 1996 in which case and control groups were interviewed in different regions of the country. The correlation between induced abortion and breast cancer was very strong in regions of the country with a predominantly Roman Catholic population, but much weaker in regions with less abortion stigma. Although the sample size of women who had abortions was small in the Catholic regions, a large number of women in those areas also underreported contraceptive use to a greater extent than in more liberal regions.

Abortion Stigma Exists in China

Anti-choice activist Dr. Joel Brind has been promoting the ABC association for over two decades. He claims that the Chinese study "neutralized" the recall bias argument. But Brind missed—or chose not to mention—that the journal article contained a confusing error, one that helped to hide the study's own recall bias shortcomings. Early on, the study authors say:

> The lack of a social stigma associated with induced abortion
> in China may limit the amount of underreporting.

But later in the study, the authors say:

[T]he self-reported number of IA [induced abortion] will probably be underestimated, as the stigma of abortion still exists in China, especially when a woman has more than two IAs. Therefore, this underestimation will inevitably create spurious associations between IA and breast cancer, especially for more IAs.

These two contradictory statements should never have gotten past the peer reviewers.

Regardless of whether abortion is stigmatized in China and to what degree, abortion is still underreported even in countries where abortion is more widely accepted, such as Estonia and Hungary. But the study authors are probably right in their second statement: Abortion stigma does exist in China. An increasing number of young unmarried women are having abortions—often multiple abortions—but there is a stigma in China against premarital sex and an even bigger stigma against out-of-wedlock pregnancies. In these circumstances, it would be very surprising indeed if young Chinese women were not underreporting their abortions. Further, since the study authors admit that abortion stigma in China is more pronounced for subsequent abortions, this would explain the rising association that the authors found between multiple abortions and breast cancer—because women in control groups would be increasingly less likely to report their second or third abortions.

Cohort Studies Are More Reliable

Another type of study, called a "cohort study," is considered more reliable than case-control studies. In a typical cohort study, researchers spend many years following large numbers of women, some of whom have had abortions, to see which ones develop breast cancer later. Recall bias is not an issue because abortion data is drawn from public records. The result

American Cancer Society Says There Is No Abortion–Breast Cancer Link

The topic of abortion and breast cancer highlights many of the most challenging aspects of studies of people and how those studies do or do not translate into public health guidelines. The issue of abortion generates passionate viewpoints in many people. Breast cancer is the most common cancer in women aside from skin cancer; and breast cancer is the second leading cancer killer in women. Still, the public is not well-served by false alarms. At this time, the scientific evidence does not support the notion that abortion of any kind raises the risk of breast cancer or any other type of cancer.

"Is Abortion Linked to Breast Cancer?,"
American Cancer Society, June 19, 2014.

is an accurate percentage of how many women got breast cancer compared to others who didn't have abortions. Out of at least nine cohort studies done since 1996, not one has found a statistically significant association between abortion and breast cancer, and some found negative associations—meaning abortion might actually protect against breast cancer.

The Chinese study was not a cohort study or even a case-control study. It was a meta-analysis, which combines the results of numerous studies on the same topic to come up with a pooled average. The authors found 36 previous Chinese studies on the ABC association and combined their results to come up with an "odds ratio" of 1.44, which means a 44 percent increased risk of breast cancer for women who had one abortion. However, the authors used 34 case-control studies and only two cohort studies (not included in the nine mentioned above). Neither cohort study showed a statistically significant ABC association. Further, six of the case-control studies that were rated as having the highest quality methodology, according to the authors' own evaluation, also showed no correlation. In other words, the supposed ABC association arose solely from the weakest 26 studies selected for the meta-analysis, some of which were not even published in peer-reviewed journals.

The major weakness of meta-analyses has a popular acronym—GIGO. It means "garbage in, garbage out." In other words, if most of the studies you add to the mix are seriously flawed, your pooled result will be worthless as well. To their credit, the study's authors make clear that induced abortion is not confirmed as a causal risk factor for breast cancer and that their own results should be interpreted with caution. In fact, the scientific community has already dismissed abortion as a risk factor based on the best studies. Given that the correlation only shows up in case-control studies but never cohort studies, it's highly likely to be an artifact of recall bias.

Other Risk Factors Explain Increase in Breast Cancer

Although correlation does not equal causation, anti-choice advocates are using the Chinese study to jump to the unwarranted conclusion that abortion causes an increased breast cancer risk. Unfortunately, the study authors never mention other possible risk factors that could help explain the recent rise in breast cancer in China, let alone why they should be rejected in favor of abortion. These include:

- Fewer full-term pregnancies (one or two) because of the one-child policy;

- Economic development leading to more affluence and rising body weight (as found in one of the two Chinese cohort studies);

- Increased industrialization and dramatically increased exposure to environmental toxins in a country with few environmental controls; and

- Improved protocols for cancer testing, leading to more diagnoses of breast cancer.

Because the study focuses only on China, it also obscures the lack of association between breast cancer and abortion in many other countries. For example, Western Europe has low abortion rates and high breast cancer rates, while Russia has high abortion rates and moderate breast cancer rates. It is unreasonable to assume the existence of an ABC association when it's found inconsistently and depends more on geography or study methodology. Further, if there really were a causal connection, it would show up more robustly across most studies, instead of being all over the map.

The study's ABC association was quite weak in comparison to major risk factors for breast cancer, such as advanced age, having a family history of breast cancer, or being childless. In a specific population such as women in China, weak associations can turn up by chance, and are therefore random and meaningless. For example, if you compared the population of storks with the rates of childbirth outside hospitals in various countries, a correlation will appear in some of them. It does not mean that storks deliver babies in some countries but not in others. It just means that you can find a correlation between almost anything if you're determined to find it.

The promotion of flawed studies to try to prove that abortion leads to breast cancer is a political effort spearheaded by anti-choice groups and individuals who primarily use these studies to reinforce abortion stigma and frighten women. The studies may also be a vehicle to smuggle in dogmatic beliefs under the guise of objectivity and the scientific method. As such, they irresponsibly advance an anti-choice agenda at the expense of science and women's welfare.

> *"Having all chilled out, let this plausible but unproven factor in the increased breast cancer rates of recent decades be given ongoing cool consideration by experts, free of ideological filters and far from the madding crowd."*

Politics Should Be Taken Out of the Abortion–Breast Cancer Debate

David van Gend

David van Gend is a family doctor in Toowoomba, Australia. In the following viewpoint, van Gend argues that there is a big difference in the tone of the debates on a potential link between vasectomy and prostate cancer and abortion and breast cancer. Neither link has been conclusively proven, yet both are worthy of further research and study. However, van Gend says, while the vasectomy–prostate cancer debate is waged politely, political and moral issues make the abortion–breast cancer debate more emotional and less scientific.

As you read, consider the following questions:

1. According to the viewpoint, what were the findings of the Lecarpentier paper as to the link between abortion and breast cancer?

2. What is the value of the scoring system proposed by the Lecarpentier paper, according to the author?

3. What advice does the author give to social progressives and social conservatives on the abortion–breast cancer controversy?

A Mexican wave of moral indignation swept through the chattering class this month [August 2014] in Australia when the hypothesis was raised of a link between abortion and breast cancer. We heard, in shrill tones, that claims of such a link are "factually incorrect" (blogger Mia Freedman), "absurd" (Simon Breheny of the IPA [Institute of Public Affairs Australia]) and even "an insult to all women" (Greens MP [member of Parliament] Adam Bandt). With the arrival this week of breast surgeon and cancer researcher Dr Angela Lanfranchi to speak to this hypothesis, we can expect a resurgence of this rage.

Prostate Cancer–Vasectomy Link Is Less Controversial

Yet no such public frenzy occurred when the closest male equivalent—a correlation between vasectomy and prostate cancer—was proposed only last month. Why is it a slur against women to consider a link between abortion and breast cancer, but no slur against men to suggest that vasectomy might be linked to prostate cancer? Both hypotheses remain unproven, plagued by conflicting evidence, yet both deal with grave medical issues that demand ongoing dispassionate research.

Consider last month's publication on prostate cancer in the *Journal of Clinical Oncology*. It was a 24-year follow-up study and concluded, "Our data support the hypothesis that vasectomy is associated with a modest increased incidence of lethal prostate cancer." Yet look back over that 24-year period and you will see that the vasectomy–prostate cancer hypothesis has waxed and waned, just like the abortion–breast cancer hypothesis.

In 1993 the *Journal of the American Medical Association* investigated the question, "Vasectomy and prostate cancer: chance, bias, or a causal relationship?" and made the point that "any causal relationship between the two would be important both for individual and public health." The same point should be calmly made about any relationship between abortion and breast cancer. A decade later, the ABC's [Australian Broadcasting Corporation's] *Health Report* commentator Dr Norman Swan exulted in newer prostate research published in the same prestigious journal, telling his male listeners, "There has been some concern about an alleged increased risk of prostate cancer after vasectomy. But recent research from New Zealand found no link between them—so the only excuse now is cowardice!"

Contrast the good-natured commentary on the prostate cancer theory to the vulgar chorus of denunciation of the breast cancer theory.

Studies Draw Differing Conclusions on Abortion–Breast Cancer Link

Yet if the link between abortion and breast cancer is not worthy of consideration, why does the question keep being raised in peer-reviewed medical journals? When four of the five largest studies on this subject in the past two years report a significant correlation, why did medical authorities stand by this month and let this inoffensive hypothesis be lynched by an ignorant mob? Worse, why did the president of the AMA [Australian Medical Association], Dr Brian Owler, do such injustice to the published research with his categorical statement, "There is no evidence to say breast cancer and abortion are linked. Let's not use false evidence or try and link abortion with other things such as breast cancer."

The truth is far more interesting, and concerning, than Dr Owler's dismissive sound bite. Pause and consider just three major studies from the last three years.

In February this year, in the journal *Cancer Causes & Control*, [Yubei] Huang et al. published "A Meta-Analysis of the Association Between Induced Abortion and Breast Cancer Risk Among Chinese Females." After analysis of 36 studies covering 14 provinces in China, the authors concluded, "Induced abortion is significantly associated with an increased risk of breast cancer among Chinese females, and the risk of breast cancer increases as the number of induced abortions increases."

By contrast, last year a large Danish study[, by Christina Marie Brauner et al., in *Acta Obstetricia et Gynecologica Scandinavica*,] investigated "Induced Abortion and Breast Cancer Among Parous Women" and concluded, "Our study did not show evidence of an association between induced abortion and breast cancer risk."

In the journal *Breast Cancer Research* in 2012, [Julie] Lecarpentier et al. investigated variation in breast cancer risk associated with factors related to pregnancies in the cohort of French women who carry the breast cancer genes BRCA1 and 2. They concluded: "We found an increased breast cancer risk associated with an increasing number of induced abortions."

Take a closer look at the Lecarpentier paper, which was a model of sober caution and acknowledged the contentious nature of this topic: "A number of studies have examined the risk of breast cancer associated with interrupted pregnancies, but there has been some controversy in the past."

After reviewing some studies with negative findings they state, "However, numerous studies have suggested that interrupted pregnancies may moderately increase the risk of breast cancer."

As with all rigorous medical research, this paper looked for a biological explanation for their positive findings. They note that completing a pregnancy prior to any subsequent abortion was strongly protective against breast cancer—which is a widely accepted finding—and postulated, "This effect may be because the differentiation of mammary cells which occurs during a full-term pregnancy prevents the carcinogenic effect of subsequent interrupted pregnancies." That hypothesis—of interrupted pregnancies being carcinogenic because they arrest breast cell development in an immature and vulnerable state, and the related finding that the cancer risk is strongly mitigated by an initial full-term pregnancy—is exactly the hypothesis Dr Lanfranchi will be discussing on her speaking tour, yet for some reason she is not accorded the same respect as the Lecarpentier team.

Finally, the French study proposes a scoring system "useful for the individual estimation of breast cancer risk" based on a number of variables such as the stage of abortion, the number of abortions, and whether there was a protective full-term pregnancy at the start. Such a scoring system would allow closer screening of higher-risk individuals, and that is a valuable tool in any cancer screening programme.

It Is Not Helpful to Breast Cancer Patients to Stifle Debate

So why would the AMA president treat with such contempt research which might help women know they are higher risk and therefore needing closer screening?

Instead he issued a ruling: "There is no link between abortion and breast cancer. We need to make that very clear to the public, and certainly we should not be promoting any papers from the 1950s."

This reference to the 1950s was in response to comments made by Senator Eric Abetz on Network Ten's *The Project*. Watch his lips as he speaks the words that lit the fuse of this month's media frenzy: "I think the studies, and I think they date back from the 1950s, assert that there is a link between abortion and breast cancer."

Abetz was correct, and if Dr Owler was so inclined he could read back through more than seventy published studies between 1957 and 2014 and find that more than three-quarters of them (of widely varying quality) assert a correlation between abortion and breast cancer. So where is the cause for offense in the senator's statement?

Abetz made clear that he was not going to make a judgment on the "factual correctness" of the hypothesis saying, "I don't have that scientific expertise," but he simply reported the fact that many studies do "assert that there is a link."

No problem with that, but his interviewer on *The Project*, Mia Freedman, pontificated, "It is conclusively and scientifically incorrect," and having closed the interview she turned to the panel and played the Holocaust card: "When people are actually having scientifically incorrect information that's incredibly disturbing. I mean, would they get up and support Holocaust deniers? This is the same thing essentially."

After Freedman's immoderate analogy, the hysteria only worsened. Her fellow blogger at *Mamamia*, Shauna Anderson, wailed: "This senator just undermined millions of breast cancer sufferers around the world." Greens MP Adam Bandt thundered, "The minister should not scare young women by peddling his dark, anti-choice ideology on national television" and demanded he apologise.

Further, Bandt stipulated that Abetz not attend the upcoming branch meeting of the World Congress of Families, a homely gathering in a church hall in suburban Melbourne this coming Sunday—free entry, bring your own tea bag— where the codirector of the Sanofi-Aventis Breast Care Center in New Jersey intends to commit a crime against humanity. Dr Lanfranchi will speak on the question of, "Induced abortion and breast cancer—is there a link and should it be a part of informed consent?"

She thinks it should because she thinks there is, and as a breast cancer expert her evidence should be listened to and argued with respectfully. The political and moral passions about abortion must not paralyse rational discussion of the purely clinical question before us.

Research and Facts Should Trump Politics

Social progressives should take a cold shower. Even if future studies confirm the abortion–breast cancer link, such a finding would not threaten the sexual revolution, or its ultimate guarantor of abortion on demand. The cancer link, if it exists, would be just another prudential calculation of risk and benefit for the patient, just like the prudential calculation of risk and benefit in using the Pill [referring to oral contraception], which we know is linked very weakly to breast cancer.

Social conservatives should take a cold shower if they think a link between abortion and breast cancer can or should be conscripted to the pro-life cause. Prudential calculations are not the stuff of moral argument. It is honourable to appeal to justice and duty in an attempt to reduce the present killing of every fourth baby in Australia; it is contemptible to appeal to the self-interest of some remote risk of cancer as a reason to let your baby live.

Having all chilled out, let this plausible but unproven factor in the increased breast cancer rates of recent decades be given ongoing cool consideration by experts, free of ideological filters and far from the madding crowd.

Periodical and Internet Sources Bibliography

The following articles have been selected to supplement the diverse views presented in this chapter.

American College of Pediatricians	"Abortion and the Risk of Breast Cancer: Information for the Adolescent Woman and Her Parents," December 2013.
Drew Belsky	"PolitiFact Gets Facts Wrong on Abortion & Breast Cancer Link," *Crisis Magazine*, June 28, 2013.
Susan Berry	"Pediatricians Warn of Abortion–Breast Cancer Link," Breitbart.com, April 17, 2015.
Joel Brind	"Abortion and Breast Cancer: The Stubborn Link Returns," *National Review Online*, March 10, 2015.
Raven Clabough	"New Study Confirms Evidence of Abortion/Breast Cancer Link," *New American*, May 5, 2014.
David A. Grimes	"Abortion and Breast Cancer: How Abortion Foes Got It Wrong," *Huffington Post*, April 27, 2015.
Billy Hallowell	"Professor Claims There's a Major Link Between Abortion and Breast Cancer That Medical Experts Are Concealing," The Blaze, December 3, 2013.
Lara Huffman	"No, Abortion Does Not Cause Breast Cancer," *Huffington Post*, October 6, 2014.
Robin Keahey	"Abortion and Breast Cancer: How Much Can We Trust Those Who Say There Is No Link?," Live Action News, September 7, 2015.
Gerard Nadal	"The Abortion Breast Cancer Link: When Orthodoxy Trumps Science and Reason," *Catholic Lane*, August 18, 2014.

OPPOSING
VIEWPOINTS®
SERIES

CHAPTER 4

Has Breast Cancer Awareness Become Commercialized?

Chapter Preface

Pink ribbons have become so ubiquitous each October, National Breast Cancer Awareness Month, that the month has been dubbed "Pinktober." Thousands of products are decorated with pink ribbons to support breast cancer awareness and fund-raising efforts. How did it begin? The history of using ribbons to raise awareness began in the nineteenth century when women wore yellow ribbons to honor men serving in the military. Tony Orlando and Dawn borrowed from this tradition when creating the 1973 song "Tie a Yellow Ribbon Round the Ole Oak Tree." Penney Laingen was inspired by this song and in 1979 began using the yellow ribbon to draw attention to the plight of her husband, Bruce Laingen, and other Americans held as hostages in Iran.

In 1991, AIDS activists decided to use the ribbon motif to draw attention to their cause. The art group Visual AIDS chose the color red for its "connection to blood and the idea of passion—not only anger, but love." The actor Jeremy Irons wore a red ribbon on his lapel to the 1992 Tony Awards, quickly establishing the red AIDS ribbon as an icon of popular culture. Also in the early 1990s, a sixty-eight-year-old breast cancer survivor, Charlotte Haley, in Simi Valley, California, launched a modest breast cancer awareness campaign from her dining room table using peach ribbons. Each ribbon was accompanied by a card saying, "The National Cancer Institute annual budget is $1.8 billion, only 5 percent goes for cancer prevention. Help us wake up our legislators and America by wearing this ribbon." Haley's efforts were largely by word of mouth; she distributed the ribbons to her local grocery stores and mailed them to prominent women.

When Alexandra Penney, the editor in chief of *SELF* magazine, learned of Haley's grassroots ribbon campaign from columnist Liz Smith, she felt it could become the focus of her magazine's second annual Breast Cancer Awareness Month is-sue. Evelyn Lauder, senior corporate vice president of Estée Lauder, who was guest editor of the issue, came up with the idea of passing out the ribbons with a breast self-exam card at Estée Lauder makeup counters. However, Haley refused to co-operate with *SELF* and Estée Lauder, citing a fear that the ini-tiative was too commercial. On the advice of their legal staffs, Penney and Lauder changed the color from peach to pink and went ahead with their campaign, inextricably linking pink rib-bons and breast cancer awareness.

The pink ribbon campaign, however, has become contro-versial. Some see it in the forefront of cause marketing. Pam Stephan, writing for About.com in August 2014, explains:

> Pink ribbons have entered politics, and changed the way corporations, legislators, and everyday people communicate their allegiance to a cause. . . . Charlotte Haley did much good, igniting a new awareness that has caused a dramatic increase in money spent on breast cancer research and pub-lic awareness campaigns.

Others say that Haley was prescient in believing that her ribbon would be exploited for commercial purposes. Accord-ing to Anna Holmes in the *Washington Post* in 2012,

> Twenty years after Haley refused the request to market her salmon-colored ribbon, pink ribbons, pink-ribboned con-sumer goods and associated runs, walks and jumps "for the cure" have become so commonplace and therefore benign that we hardly notice them; we're anesthetized to this major killer of women to the point that it's almost accepted as a rite of passage, not a profoundly painful experience. The color has been promoted as fashionable, a shorthand for a sort of optimism and positivity . . . that threatens to obscure much of the justifiable grief, frustration and fear that ac-company the epidemic, not to mention the hypocrisies of the companies who benefit from it.

In the chapter that follows, medical professionals, commentators, and other writers offer their perspectives on the commercialization of breast cancer awareness.

> *"Though breast cancer researchers and advocates perpetually plead for more money, the disease is, in fact, awash in it."*

Some Businesses and Nonprofits Exploit Breast Cancer for Profit

Lea Goldman

Lea Goldman is features and special projects director at Marie Claire *magazine. In the following viewpoint, Goldman states that more than $6 billion is raised each year for breast cancer awareness campaigns and research, and that a number of unscrupulous businesses and nonprofits have made a good deal of money from the campaigns. She says that despite all the money going to the disease, researchers are no closer to a cure than they were in the early 1990s. Many complain that too much money goes to awareness and too little to research, Goldman reports. She advises readers to avoid all pink ribbon merchandise and investigate charities carefully before donating to them.*

As you read, consider the following questions:

1. According to Goldman, how many new cases of breast cancer are diagnosed annually worldwide?

2. What are some of the breast cancer organizations that the author recommends?

3. What four questions does Goldman recommend that individuals ask before donating to a breast cancer charity?

Aside from the slow-rolling hot dogs at concession stands and the sideline billboards for Hubba Bubba bubble gum, you'd be hard-pressed to find a hint of pink at any of the National Football League's [NFL's] 31 stadiums, where, during most of the six-month season, the decor tends to match the distinctly masculine nature of the game. Not so in October, when pink becomes the de facto color of the sport. Players bound onto the field sporting pink cleats, wristbands, and chin straps, and punt pigskins emblazoned with pink decals under the watchful eyes of refs with pink whistles. It's all part of the league's massive sponsorship of National Breast Cancer Awareness Month, which by October's end will have seen the distribution of 650,000 pink ribbons at stadiums across the country.

Though the NFL has, shall we say, a *complicated* history with women, its embrace of breast cancer awareness is perhaps only fitting. After all, in the nearly 20 years since the pink ribbon became the official symbol of the cause—Estée Lauder cosmetics counters handed out 1.5 million of them in 1992 as part of the first-ever nationwide awareness campaign to leverage the pink ribbon—breast cancer has become the NFL of diseases, glutted with corporate sponsorships, merchandise deals, and ad campaigns. This is true year-round, but especially in October, when breast cancer marketing reaches a frothy pink frenzy. This month, an awareness-minded consumer can buy almost any knickknack or household item in pink—from lint brushes and shoelaces to earbuds and Snuggies. If she happens to be in an American Airlines Admirals Club, she can snack on pink cookies while drinking pink champagne. If instead she finds herself at one of the nation's 500 Jersey Mike's Subs franchises, for about $7 she can order the "pink ribbon combo," consisting of a sandwich, chips, and soda served in a limited-edition pink plastic cup (because nothing says "cancer awareness" like chips and soda).

More Money Raised for Breast Cancer than Any Other Cancer

Though breast cancer researchers and advocates perpetually plead for more money, the disease is, in fact, awash in it. Last year [2010], the National Institutes of Health, the nation's top agency for health-related research, allocated $763 million to the study of breast cancer, more than double what it committed to any other cancer. The Department of Defense also funds breast cancer research ($150 million this year), as do several states, most notably Texas and California. All that is in addition to the money raised by the roughly 1,400 IRS [Internal Revenue Service]–recognized, tax-exempt charities in this country devoted to breast cancer. They operate in every state and in just about every major city. The largest of them, Dallas-based Susan G. Komen, grossed $420 million last year alone. All told, an estimated $6 billion is raised every year in the name of breast cancer. And the money keeps pouring in.

Which seems like great news for the fight against breast cancer, and in part it is (though not as great as it sounds, and we'll get back to that). But it's also been a boon for charity scammers—the charlatans who prey on the public's beneficence and its inveterate laziness when it comes to due diligence. The nonprofit world is full of them. (Greg Mortenson, the celebrated author of *Three Cups of Tea*, is only the latest philanthropist to battle allegations that his organization, the

Central Asia Institute, misused funds.) Breast cancer makes a particularly alluring target—not just because there is so much money involved or because women across all income levels tend to give more than men, but because we give to breast cancer forcefully, eagerly, superstitiously. Breast cancer holds a peculiarly powerful sway with us—it's a disease dreaded so profoundly that not supporting the cause feels like tempting fate.

When our minds wander to the unthinkable, breast cancer tops that black list of God-help-me scenarios, conjuring up images of surgery, mutilation, chemotherapy and its attendant nausea, and hair loss (as terrifying as losing a breast for some); of helpless partners convincing us (and themselves) that we're still as desirable as before; of living with a constant, insidious fear that it's never really over. It's about our breasts, for chrissake, the embodiment of femininity, sex appeal, and motherhood. It is a disease of agonizing choices (Christina Applegate's preventive double mastectomy) and unfathomable compromises (Elizabeth Edwards' deathbed denouement with her wayward husband). This is what breast cancer means to many women, and it's why, unlike even ovarian or uterine cancer, it makes us suckers for every pink ribbon trinket and walkathon solicitation that crosses our paths.

We Are No Closer to a Cure Today

In this environment, it's difficult to ask questions. "You know, breast cancer has been untouchable for a while. If you question anything, well then, you must hate women," says Gayle Sulik, author of *Pink Ribbon Blues*. "That mentality makes it really hard to say, 'What's working? What's not working?' The goal is eradication. Isn't that what we say we want?" There is no denying that money raised for research has been instrumental in the fight against breast cancer. Sophisticated digital mammography has reduced the risk of false-positive diagnoses; the discovery of genetic markers has allowed women with increased risk for breast cancer to weigh their preventive options early; drugs like Herceptin, which targets the proteins responsible for a cancer cell's growth, have demonstrated remarkable results in the 20 percent of patients afflicted with the particularly aggressive HER2-positive form of breast cancer. Doctors warn that there are never any absolutes when it comes to breast cancer, but for the 60 percent of women diagnosed at the earliest stage, survival is virtually guaranteed.

Yet what many in the breast cancer community are loath to admit, despite all these lifesaving developments, is that, in fact, we are really no closer to a cure today than we were two decades ago. In 1991, 119 women in the U.S. died of breast cancer every day. Today, that figure is 110—a victory no one is bragging about. Breast cancer remains the leading cancer killer among women ages 20 to 59; more than 1.4 million new cases are diagnosed annually worldwide. Roughly 5 percent, or 70,000, breast cancer patients are diagnosed at a late stage, after the cancer has metastasized—that rate hasn't budged since 1975, despite all the medical advances and awareness campaigns. For these women, the prognosis remains grim: Only 1 in 5 will survive five years out. Fundamental questions still elude researchers: Why do a third of all women considered cured by their doctors suffer recurrences? Why are breast cancer rates rising in Asia, where they've been historically low? Is it even possible to prevent breast cancer, and if so, how?

Sham Charities Profit from Breast Cancer

A popular gripe among advocates is that too much is spent on awareness campaigns—walks, races, rallies—at the expense of research. (And really, when Snuggies go pink, haven't we hit our awareness saturation point?) There's a case to be made for that, of course, but there's another explanation, one that exposes an ugly, even blasphemous, truth of the movement: Breast cancer has made a lot of people very wealthy. The fact is, thousands of people earn a handsome living extending their proverbial pink tin cups, baiting their benefactors with the promise of a cure, as if one were realistically in sight. They divert press, volunteers, and public interest away from other, more legitimate organizations, to say nothing of the money they raise, which, despite the best intentions of donors, doesn't always go where it's supposed to.

In 2001, Hillary Rutter received a call at her Plainview, Long Island, home from an outfit called the Plainview Chapter of the Coalition Against Breast Cancer [CABC], asking for a contribution to help subsidize the medical expenses of local breast cancer survivors.

Rutter, the director of the Adelphi New York Statewide Breast Cancer Hotline & Support Program, had never heard of the group and didn't know any of its board members. When she asked pointed questions about where donations were going, the caller hung up on her. Three weeks later, she received an invoice from the CABC stating that she'd pledged $25.

Galled that a fly-by-night operation would exploit the issue of breast cancer in Long Island, where women have long suspected they are at an epicenter of the disease, Rutter secured a copy of the group's financial records. (Tax returns of nonprofits are available to the public.) What she saw shocked her: Breast cancer patients saw virtually nothing from the $1 million the group had raised. Instead, those dollars went to telemarketers and salaries. Rutter began keeping a file on the group, which over the years grew thick with complaints about harassing calls and questionable fund-raising tactics. "As far as I know, the CABC has done nothing but line their own pockets," says Rutter. "They're just horrible."

Last June, New York attorney general Eric Schneiderman filed suit against the Coalition Against Breast Cancer, calling it a "sham charity" that for 15 years "served as a personal piggy bank" for the group's insiders. According to the complaint, founder Andrew Smith; his girlfriend, Debra Koppelman; and their associates pilfered almost all of the $9.1 million raised in the past five years alone. Other eye-opening claims: The telemarketing firm hired to solicit donations was owned by CABC cofounder Garrett Morgan, who billed the charity $3.5 million for his services. In total, Smith and Koppelman paid themselves more than $550,000 in salaries between 2005 and 2009, plus another $150,000 in retirement accounts, this though both held down full-time jobs as recruiters. The CABC issued Smith a $105,000 personal loan, which he squandered on bad investments; Koppelman authorized a $50,000 loan to herself toward the purchase of a home. (CABC is contesting these claims.)

"There is a lot of deception that goes on with breast cancer groups," says Daniel Borochoff, president of the American Institute of Philanthropy, a Chicago-based nonprofit watchdog group. One problem, he says, is that breast cancer charities are often run by well-meaning but inexperienced survivors or relatives who duplicate the efforts of established organizations. They use donor dollars to print their own educational brochures, though they certainly exist elsewhere; they organize events to promote awareness—"Skydive to End Breast Cancer!"—then blow too much of their funds getting these events off the ground. There's no requirement of a college degree or business experience to run a charity. You don't even need a clean legal record. (The treasurer for the Coalition Against Breast Cancer was a Long Island housepainter with several warrants for unpaid child support.) Even the names of many charities are designed to fool donors into believing they are bigger and more impressive than they are. Case in point: Though its moniker suggests it presides over a vast network, the Breast Cancer Charities of America is a tiny, three-woman outfit operating just outside Houston that banked $2 million in 2009, mostly through telemarketers. (Founder Erica Harvey says she came up with the name "with a team of marketing consultants.") "Any bozo can set up [a charity] and start soliciting," adds Borochoff.

All charities must file detailed financial reports with the Internal Revenue Service, but they don't have to be audited, or certified by a licensed accountant. In effect, anyone can write them up and turn them in. Some states require that a CPA [certified public accountant] review the books, but the rules vary widely. In California, only groups grossing $2 million or more per year need a CPA's certification; there's no auditing requirement at all in Texas. Even still, it's alarmingly easy to boost a charity's numbers to make it appear as if it's spending more on its mission—education and support groups, for example—than it actually is, especially for the many nonprofit outfits that rely on telemarketing. Here's how it's done: If a telemarketer charges, say, 70 cents for every dollar it collects—telemarketers are as expensive as they are annoying—a charity can write off some of that expense as part of its educational mandate by stamping "Don't forget to get a mammogram!" at the bottom of its invoices to donors. Another common accounting trick allows charities to accept gifts—say, a used car worth $500—but then report these contributions at a much higher value. Neither tactic is illegal, by the way. What's the point of all this financial monkey business? Size matters when it comes to charities. The bigger the organization, the more reputable it seems, and the more likely it is to receive your cash. . . .

Avoid Pink Ribbon Merchandise

The net result of all this profiteering? Pink has lost its punch. "All these groups that have sprouted up around the country have diffused the attention to breast cancer," contends Fran Visco, president of the National Breast Cancer Coalition and former chair of the integration panel of the Department of Defense Breast Cancer Research Program. "They take up dollars and put them into little pots all across the country. They take away from the efforts that can—and do—make a differ-

Cancer-Causing Businesses Join the Breast Cancer Cult

By ignoring or underemphasizing the vexing issue of environmental causes, the breast cancer cult turns women into dupes of what could be called the Cancer Industrial Complex: the multinational corporate enterprise that with the one hand doles out carcinogens and disease and, with the other, offers expensive, semi-toxic pharmaceutical treatments. Breast Cancer Awareness Month, for example, is sponsored by AstraZeneca (the manufacturer of tamoxifen), which, until a corporate reorganization in 2000, was a leading producer of pesticides, including acetochlor, classified by the EPA [Environmental Protection Agency] as a "probable human carcinogen." This particularly nasty conjuncture of interests led the environmentally oriented Cancer Prevention Coalition (CPC) to condemn Breast Cancer Awareness Month as "a public relations invention by a major polluter which puts women in the position of being unwitting allies of the very people who make them sick.". . .

In the harshest judgment, the breast cancer cult serves as an accomplice in global poisoning—normalizing cancer, prettying it up, even presenting it, perversely, as a positive and enviable experience.

Barbara Ehrenreich,
"Welcome to Cancerland: A Mammogram Leads
to a Cult of Pink Kitsch," Harper's, November 2001.

ence. They should all be focused on putting themselves out of business." But who closes up shop when business is booming?

For anyone worried about where their donations are going, here's a useful tip: Skip the pink ribbon merchandise. Because no one really owns the rights to what has become the universal symbol of breast cancer (though Susan G. Komen trademarked its own version), peddling the logo has become a massive racket, overrun by slick profiteers exploiting the public's naive assumption that all pink purchases help the cause. Often they don't. Tchotchke vendor Oriental Trading sells an extensive line of pink ribbon party favors, including "Find the cure" car magnets and "I wear pink in honor of" buttons. Save for proceeds from its pink rubber duckies, part of a sponsorship deal with Komen, not a penny of Oriental Trading's breast cancer novelties goes to breast cancer. Three years ago, veteran nurse Christina McCall, the daughter of a breast cancer survivor, launched Pink Ribbon Marketplace, an online store based in Germantown, Tennessee, with a vast array of pink-hued goodies. "As a woman and the mother of three daughters, it quickly became apparent that creating a business that gives back to breast cancer victims and their families was important to me," she writes on her store's website. "I personally chose our local American Cancer Society and Reach to Recovery program to be the receipient [sic] of funds we donate." But when asked about those donations, McCall fesses up that, in fact, no monies have ever gone to the American Cancer Society or its breast-cancer-targeted Reach to Recovery program. "I'm a little leery of [donating money]," McCall told Marie Claire [MC]. Instead, she says she gives away free products to charity events and donates to individuals—"depending on my profits." (Shortly after MC contacted her, McCall removed any reference to the American Cancer Society from her website.)

Last year, the Better Business Bureau [BBB] issued a warning to consumers about misleading or vague claims made on the packaging of pink ribbon–festooned products. "Simply because a company puts a pink ribbon on its package doesn't always mean a good breast cancer charity is benefiting from your purchase," noted Michelle L. Corey, a BBB exec.

Google "pink ribbon," and the first listing to pop up is pinkribbon.com, the glossy website of Pink Ribbon International, an Amsterdam-based outfit owned by Dutch businessman Walter Scheffrahn. The site serves up an eclectic mix of breast cancer information and merchandise, including a yard sign ($14.99) and barbecue apron ($16.99) embossed with the site's logo. Over the past seven years, Scheffrahn has shelled out 200,000 euro ($288,000) to buy the rights to the enviable pinkribbon.com domain name in roughly 40 countries. "There's not a real global awareness of the pink ribbon," says Scheffrahn. "We want to take it to the next stage." But despite its official-looking packaging, his site is riddled with misleading information, including a statement that Scheffrahn's company donates "10 percent of its company capacity and funds" to charity. Exactly how much is that? Scheffrahn says it refers to manpower, not actual dollars. Scheffrahn also claims that 90 percent of donations made to breast cancer through his websites go to charity. (Ten percent is reserved for overhead, he says.) But this, as it turns out, is also a bit fuzzy. Scheffrahn says his entire web network generated "something like $20,000" by the end of last year. (That's hard to confirm given that, at press time, pinkribbon.com's tax returns were not yet available to the public.) So where did the $20,000 go? Scheffrahn confesses that not only hasn't he donated the money yet, he's unsure which organization to give it to. "It will go to a fund we think is appropriate," is all he can come up with, as though it were the first time he'd ever been asked the question.

Where Should You Give?

These well-regarded breast cancer organizations spend most of their funds on research and treatment:

- Breast Cancer Research Foundation
- Memorial Sloan Kettering Cancer Center
- The University of Texas, MD Anderson Cancer Center
- Dana-Farber Cancer Institute
- The Johns Hopkins Avon Foundation Breast Center . . .

Think Before You Pink

Not all pink ribbons benefit breast cancer. Before you buy anything to support "the fight against breast cancer", ask these key questions:

How much money from the purchase actually goes toward breast cancer programs and services?

Can you tell? If the company selling the merchandise says "a portion of proceeds," find out how much exactly. (The packaging or label ought to make this explicit.) Also, is there a cap on how much the company will donate to charity in total? Some companies will give a set donation, regardless of your purchase.

Where is the money going?

What organization will get the money? If you can't tell or you don't know what the organization does, reconsider your purchase.

What types of programs are being supported?

If research, what kind? If services, are they reaching the people who need them most? Be wary of programs supporting "breast cancer awareness"—what exactly does that mean? How are they making consumers aware?

Is the product itself not contributing to the breast cancer epidemic?

In 2010, Susan G. Komen controversially partnered with KFC [Kentucky Fried Chicken] on a "Buckets for the Cure" campaign, which promptly inspired howls from breast cancer advocates who argued that fatty foods like fried chicken actually raise your risk for breast cancer.

> *"Breast cancer awareness has long been the poster child for what's known as 'cause marketing.'"*

Businesses Buy into Breast Cancer Awareness

Jacob Kanclerz and Ben Sutherly

Jacob Kanclerz is an executive branch reporter for Michigan Information & Research Service. Ben Sutherly is a reporter for the Columbus Dispatch in Ohio. In the following viewpoint, Kanclerz and Sutherly argue that breast cancer awareness is an easy issue for businesses to support. Both large enterprises such as the National Football League (NFL) and Kroger, as well as small local businesses, are getting on the breast cancer bandwagon, the reporters note. They conclude that by providing support for a popular cause, businesses are deepening their relationships with their customers.

As you read, consider the following questions:

1. According to the viewpoint, what is "cause marketing"?

2. What percentage of Americans want businesses they patronize to support causes, according to a study by Cone Communications?

3. What percentage of mothers were likely to switch brands for a cause they support, according to a study by Cone Communications?

It's the latest indication of local business partnerships popping up to raise awareness of breast cancer: signs reserving spaces for breast cancer survivors in the parking lots of seven local shopping centers.

During October, which has been designated Breast Cancer Awareness Month, dozens of parking spaces are reserved in shopping centers owned by developer Casto. The 48 signs read "Reserved for Breast Cancer Survivor" and have an emblem for the Arthur G. James Cancer Hospital.

Breast cancer survivors do not need documentation to use the spots, which are available on the honor system, said Theresa DiNardo Brown, a James spokeswoman.

Casto also allows the cancer hospital to place messages encouraging women to get a "James mammogram" on the stripes in its parking lots and to place banners on utility poles and other highly visible places on its properties at no cost to the hospital. There are 670 parking lot messages at Casto shopping centers.

The hospital is seeing record mammography numbers, "and we believe it's due in large measure to going out to where those women are," DiNardo Brown said.

Several businesses, small and large, have joined the effort to raise awareness of breast cancer.

The National Football League will display flashes of pink on its teams' uniforms throughout the month. Cincinnati-based Kroger is spreading the word, as are some of the brands it sells, including Pepsi and Kraft.

Grateful for Breast Cancer Awareness Month

Since my diagnosis, I am thankful to [have lived] through 10 Octobers as Breast Cancer Awareness Month. . . . So, bring it on—all 31 days—as patients and advocates use their narratives to educate about breast cancer and its risks to improve prevention, screening, treatment, and research outcomes.

Nancy M. Cappello, "Bring It On:
October 2015 Breast Cancer Awareness Month,"
Huffington Post, *November 3, 2014.*

Many companies say getting in on the awareness effort makes sound business sense. Breast cancer awareness has long been the poster child for what's known as "cause marketing"—corporate support for an issue through promotions and partnerships, often with nonprofit groups that work for that particular cause.

Marketing analysts say supporting causes helps develop better relationships with customers.

"It's not so much of a sales tactic as it a marketing tactic for longtime loyalty," said Chris Boring, a retail analyst with Boulevard Strategies.

According to a 2010 study by the public relations and marketing firm Cone Communications, 83 percent of Americans want businesses they patronize to support causes. Breast cancer awareness is a relatively easy issue to support, said Alison DaSilva, executive vice president with Cone Communications. It's well-established, and, more important, it's not a polarizing issue, she said.

Tom Santor, a spokesman for Donatos, said backing efforts to boost breast cancer awareness means not having to spend time and money explaining the cause.

"We can jump right into trying to raise funds for the cause instead of having to do a lot of education," Santor said.

Donatos raised $42,000 last year [2011] for the Stefanie Spielman Fund for Breast Cancer Research, which benefits the James. The chain's 62 central Ohio locations plan to top that this year. Local Kroger stores this month are donating some of the proceeds from sales of pink-labeled food products, plus all the proceeds from some merchandise—pink ribbons, balloons and light bulbs—to Komen Columbus and the James, said Jackie Siekmann, spokeswoman for Kroger.

"We see people gravitate toward the pink boxes," she said. Across the company, Kroger has raised $25 million in the past five years for its October initiatives. The Columbus division has raised $2.2 million in the past four years for its October promotions.

Dublin-based builder Epcon Communities donates $1,000 to Komen Columbus for each condo that goes into contract.

Many Epcon homeowners are women, said Nanette Overly, the company's vice president for sales and marketing. "It was just a very natural fit," Overly said.

The Cone Communications study showed that 93 percent of mothers were likely to switch brands for a cause they support. Epcon, which has taken part in fund-raising since 2009, donated $6,000 last year and hopes an improving housing market will help it double its local fund-raising total this year, she said.

DaSilva said transparency is crucial: Customers should look at where the money is going. She recommends that businesses be up-front about those with whom they partner and how much they give.

| *"We always feel like we're racing. We re-
  ally are racing for the cure."*

The Komen Foundation Uses Savvy Marketing to Fight Breast Cancer

Nancy Brinker interviewed by Philanthropy *magazine*

Nancy Brinker is the founder and chair of global strategy of Su-san G. Komen, a nonprofit breast cancer organization. She is also the World Health Organization's goodwill ambassador for cancer control. In the following viewpoint, Brinker explains that Susan G. Komen is one of the world's largest cancer charities, dedicating its efforts to breast cancer research, community health, advocacy, and global reach. Brinker credits her time at Neiman Marcus and her association with Stanley Marcus with giving her an appreciation of private-sector marketing, which she was able to use at Komen. Although there is still no cure for breast cancer, Brinker is proud of the research Komen has funded that has brought about advances such as the understanding of genetic susceptibility to breast cancer.

As you read, consider the following questions:

1. According to Brinker, how many people participate in the Susan G. Komen Race for the Cure 5K run annually?

2. How much money did the Komen organization spend on cancer research in 2010, according to Brinker?

3. What were some of the obstacles that Brinker describes in establishing the Komen organization?

Nancy Brinker divides her life into 13-minute increments. That's how long it takes breast cancer to kill another woman. 13 minutes. A four-year-old boy loses his mother. 13 minutes. Nine children lose their grandmother. 13 minutes. A college student loses her older sister. For years, Nancy Brinker has been racing to lengthen the intervals. And she won't stop until they go away forever.

Inspiration from Her Sister's Battle

The clock started for Nancy in 1977. Her older sister, Susan, was diagnosed with breast cancer. Susan was a mother of two, a homecoming queen and model. Her diagnosis was not the sort of thing that people felt comfortable talking about. "Promise me it'll be better," Susan asked her sister. "Breast cancer—we have to talk about it. It has to change . . . so women know . . . so they won't die." "I promise, Suzy. I swear," Nancy replied. "Even if it takes the rest of my life." Susan died three years later, at the age of 36.

And so Nancy began the race of a lifetime. In 1982, she founded the Susan G. Komen Breast Cancer Foundation, now known as Susan G. Komen for the Cure (SGK) [in 2015 known as Susan G. Komen]. The organization planned to raise money from sponsors, corporate partners, and signature events and then direct the proceeds to cancer research, advocacy, and prevention. In 1983, it held its first Race for the Cure, in Dallas. A year later, Nancy herself battled breast cancer—and won.

Today, SGK ranks among the world's largest and best-known cancer charities. In countries around the world, it hosts Race for the Cure 5K runs and walks—over 140 to date. Every year, more than 1.6 million people participate. In the United States, races are organized by local Komen affiliates, and 75 percent of the funds raised from the race go to breast cancer education, screening, treatment, and outreach programs in that community. (The remainder goes to the national organization to support breast cancer research.) In 2010, the Race for the Cure alone raised nearly $180 million. That same year, the national Komen organization spent over $280 million on cancer research, screening, treatment, and education.

As Nancy worked to scale up SGK, she often called on an accomplished entrepreneur: her husband, Norman Brinker. Brinker pioneered casual dining chain restaurants, starting with Steak and Ale in the 1960s. In 1984, [he] took over Chili's, then a small Texas restaurant chain with a few dozen locations. Before his death in 2009, Brinker had grown it to more than 1,400 locations worldwide. During his lifetime, his firm, Brinker International, was also the parent company of Romano's Macaroni Grill, Maggiano's Little Italy, and Corner Bakery [Cafe]; the firm's income grew to $220 million in 2007.

In 2001, Nancy Brinker left her seat on SGK's board to serve for two years as ambassador to Hungary. From 2007 to 2009, she served as chief of protocol of the United States, working to ensure the proper diplomatic interaction of American and foreign leaders. Since 2008, she has also served on the board of the John F. Kennedy Center for the Performing Arts. In 2009, she assumed her current post as CEO [chief executive officer] of Susan G. Komen for the Cure, and President Barack Obama awarded her the Presidential Medal of Freedom.

Philanthropy spoke with Amb. Brinker over tea and cookies at her residence in Georgetown.

Marketing Is About Telling a Story

PHILANTHROPY: Before we talk about Susan G. Komen for the Cure, can you tell me a little about your business background?

AMB. BRINKER: Of course. I graduated from college and went to live in Dallas, Texas. I was employed by one of very few companies that had executive-track openings for women: Neiman Marcus. I wasn't particularly interested in clothes and fashion, but I was very interested in marketing. Stanley Marcus—who was the son of the founder, and one of the greatest retailers ever known to mankind—had an enormous influence on me.

What do you remember most about your time there?

Mr. Marcus taught me that you always have to create the experience—always tell the customer a story, always make the merchandise look fresh. With him, there was always excitement and drama and high visibility. He was constantly bringing the customer new experiences—and he never stopped selling. He taught me a sense of urgency: you never stop selling. I just absorbed lessons from him. I watched every single thing he did very carefully.

He was always "telling a story"? What does that mean, and how important is it?

Utterly important. We do it at Komen for the Cure—every survivor's story, every family member's story, is what drives our organization and our mission.

Why is it so important? Well, a story gives meaning to whatever you do. I think of my collection of Hungarian art. It goes from 1866 to the present day, and it's purposely broken down into periods of the Austro-Hungarian Empire, the interwar period, post–World War II. The art is beautiful, but it is especially meaningful to me because of the collection's story.

You see, I started collecting when I was ambassador. It allowed me to see the Hungarians' country. I wanted to know about the country. I could not learn the language—it's very difficult. The only way I could really understand the country was through the art. Then I began to love the art, because I started seeing it through the artists' eyes, so I hope to be able to chronicle the contemporary part of it. I exhibited a lot of these pictures in the American embassy because I came right around 9/11 [referring to the September 11, 2001, terrorist attacks on the United States], and there wasn't a way to get American art into our embassy there—they weren't sending things of value out of the country. So it became a great handshake with the Hungarians when I exhibited their contemporary art in our embassy.

But back to your point, stories are indeed absolutely central to communicating what we're most passionate about.

Learning Team Building from Her Husband

You mentioned Stanley Marcus. Who else has influenced the way you think about marketing and business?

My father has been a huge influence in my life. He was a small businessman, and, before that, a traveling salesman. My father was a very hard worker—he worked his way up to developing shopping centers. He was very successful in Peoria, Illinois, where I grew up. He used to say, "Most people fail not because they have a bad idea, but because they quit."

And then, of course, I was married to a genius in Norman Brinker, who was the father of casual dining restaurants. From Norman I learned team building. He was a great listener. He was a great inspirational person, a great motivator. And to him, running his business was a little bit like putting together a football team. He wanted people to feel like they were on the team—not to feel that they were just employed but rather that they were part of the success of the business. I watched how Norman built concept after concept, tinkering with them so that they were really running before they were exported to another city or town—which is what we did with the Race for the Cure.

My only sister, Suzy, died in 1980. It was the biggest heartache of my life. Before she died, she told me, "Promise me it'll be better for women with breast cancer. . . . Promise you'll make it change." Norman knew of my sadness about my sister's death and the promise I had made, and he said, "Well, why don't you start an organization?"

In those days, there was practically nothing like this for women diagnosed with breast cancer. It just wasn't possible to talk about it. That was the challenge. How do you market or sell something that people can't even talk about? If there is anything positive in this, how do you bring people to it so they can feel good? How do you bring them together and create hope?

You must have faced enormous obstacles.

Oh, certainly. Very little research was being directed from the National Cancer Institute [NCI] to breast cancer research or to any targeted women's diseases. It was thought that cancer is a disease that you study generally. Most people equated cancer with death, or at least with a lot of disfigurement, and many were more afraid of the treatment than the disease. Also, advocacy movements still scared people. They don't quite know how to join. In our case, they didn't want to go to any more sit-ins—they had already done that in college during the Vietnam War.

People wanted to know if they could actually do something for a cause.

And that's what I think we offered at Susan G. Komen. We offered a way for people to come together to communicate their feelings, to bring their stories to the table. This was a very personal reach to someone. "Come and share your story," we said. "Come and talk to me. Tell us where you're hurting and what you need to know. Let us help you find the resources."

Applying Private-Sector Marketing

It sounds as if you were applying the lessons you learned from Stanley Marcus about "creating an experience."

Yes, I think that's right. I saw this very clearly after spending all the time I did at Neiman Marcus and watching how private-sector marketing works. We've got to deliver the message in ways that people can receive it. They weren't getting it from TV, from magazines, from newspapers—they wouldn't even print the word "breast!" That had never been done in a public setting before. Then, you went to a physician. The physician told you what to do, but you didn't call a hotline, and you sure as heck didn't go into town hall meetings and talk about your breast cancer. Breast cancer, like all cancers, was called the "Big C."

In fact, there was very little private philanthropy going to breast cancer. Using private philanthropy to find a cure—how I envisioned Susan G. Komen—was an outgrowth of my experience as a child. Along with our mother, Suzy and I were very involved in the March of Dimes, the national campaign to eradicate polio. At the time, people were quarantined when they got polio. When we saw our little friends again, many were disfigured. Sometimes they would die. We watched the whole nation galvanize around fighting a disease: the private sector, the public sector, your teachers, your doctors, your postal workers. You could hardly walk out of the front door without a March of Dimes lady saying, "I need your dimes!" In 1955, the day that Jonas Salk's vaccine was announced, the factories in Peoria shut down. The church bells were ringing. The principal got on the loudspeaker and we were all sent home. It was as if a war had ended. And it had. We had a vaccine.

But we've not achieved a polio-style victory over breast cancer.

No. I thought when we started this that we would have this done in 10 years. That's how young, naive, and silly I was.

We had put a man on the moon, and President [Richard] Nixon had launched the "war on cancer" in 1971. So by the time we had started Komen, I thought, *piece of cake.*

Komen has touched many—if not most—of the scientific advances in breast cancer since we started in 1982. We've supported the understanding of genetic susceptibility to breast cancer, including the BRCA1 and BRCA2 gene mutations, the development of treatment and prevention therapies for hormone-dependent breast cancer, the identification of HER2-positive breast cancer and the development of HER2-targeted therapies. We're supporting new work developing breast cancer vaccines, searching for biomarkers, and on and on and on. We've funded over 2,000 scientists since we started. We're the largest private funder of breast cancer research in the world.

Proudest of Research Advances

Which of these advances stands out to you?

Well, there's BRCA1, the breast cancer susceptibility gene 1, carried by 1 in 200 women, who have a lifetime risk of 60 to 90 percent for developing breast cancer. For me, it was a bittersweet experience because I'm BRCA positive. I'm sure my sister was, too. But it has been an amazing discovery. Not only have we funded a study of BRCA as a genetic base for describing who might be more at risk for breast cancer, it's also going to serve as a basic understanding of how we develop treatments for one of the most aggressive kinds of breast cancer: triple-negative disease, which doesn't respond to either hormonal treatments like tamoxifen or inhibitors like Herceptin.

Our research program overall has been a real star. This year [2011], we've given away $66 million in funding for research. As of this year, we've funded almost $700 million in research. We like to make big investments in several areas now. For many years, we largely funded cancer biology. Now we are funding cancer biology and cancer treatment, prevention, early detection, and disparities in breast cancer outcomes.

Most of the research we fund is translational, meaning that it connects findings from basic, laboratory-based scientific research into medical advancements, medical practice. We've invested $2 million with Indiana University, funding the Susan G. Komen for the Cure IU Tissue Bank, where healthy breast tissue is being carefully digitized so any pathologist around the world can use it. We've funded $84 million in Promise Grants, which are large, multiyear grants that work across different disciplines and even across different institutions on big issues. Those are the kinds of things we do. We like to go and fund the people doing this research.

What about grants that, for whatever reason, don't pan out as expected?

I don't think there is anything we have invested in that was a complete flop, that left us feeling embarrassed. We have been pretty fleet of foot—if something isn't working, we just move on. We just don't feel we are an organization that should be funding things ad infinitum. And we really like to fund people who need that one, early boost.

Do you think that research funded by private philanthropy is more independent? Does it have more freedom of action than that funded by the government?

Sometimes it does, sure. Researchers often do not feel held up by us. They know they have a little more freedom, and they might be given an opportunity to let their study take an unexpected turn. Whereas if they are taking a government grant, an NCI grant, it would be a very different thing. Our grants allow for a more visionary quality, I think.

Plus, they're now going to be in a very august group of people who are able to then shape the next chapter of what they're doing. That's very exciting for scientists. Nobody likes

Marketing a Hopeful Message About Breast Cancer

The story of Komen [referring to the Susan G. Komen organization] is, as much as anything, a story of savvy marketing. Ms. [Nancy] Brinker has rebranded an entire disease by putting an upbeat spin on fighting it. Her foundation generated about $420 million in the 2010 fiscal year alone. Perhaps more than any other nonprofit organization, Komen shapes the national conversation about breast cancer.

If you're feeling hopeful about the strides being made against this disease, rather than frustrated by the lack of progress, that may well reflect Komen's handiwork. If you think women should be concerned about developing breast cancer, that's often Komen's message, too. And if you think mammography is the best answer at the moment, that, again, is the Komen mantra.

Natasha Singer,
"Welcome, Fans, to the Pinking of America,"
New York Times, *October 15, 2011.*

to do science in a vacuum. Scientists like to communicate and collaborate. Incidentally, that's a problem for a lot of corporate research.

Doesn't collaboration take place with for-profit researchers?

Not always. Sometimes the private sector is reluctant to share its findings—they don't want to share data, for understandable reasons.

Supporting Programs at the Local Level

Apart from research, what else does Komen fund?

Research is one of the four pillars that hold up our Susan G. Komen house. The other three are community health, advocacy, and global reach. Last year, research accounted for about a quarter of our mission spending, or $75 million. We spent about half of our mission funds on education, and the rest on screening and treatment programs.

On the community health front, for example, in Montgomery County, Maryland, we helped shorten the length of a diagnostic procedure. Women were getting mammograms through a community program we do, but it was taking sometimes as long as 110 days for them to get follow-up. We shortened the follow-up period to less than a week.

I think a lot of people tend to think about us in terms of events like the Race for the Cure and icons like the pink ribbon. That's because of our affiliate network—where we're in the communities. Thanks to our affiliates across the country and around the world, we're able to offer these kinds of community health programs. Whether they are working for the organization or one of our tens of thousands of volunteers, everybody is working for this mission. And when you see the results, when you see the power of what we can do—well, that's the sexy part of working here.

How does having local affiliates fit into your overarching goals?

All health care is really local, and that's key to this effort. Some people can go to regional cancer centers throughout the country, but by and large, most people receive their health care locally. I think our organization has thrived because we understand how to train people at the local level, to create awareness and successful programs, and then how to build programs to raise money to get people to volunteer, to keep them affiliated with the cause. And even though we are sometimes criticized after the month of October [National Breast Cancer Awareness Month] for saturating everything in pink, it's very deliberate. Make no mistake, it is deliberate. Pink isn't about selling products. It's the power of millions of people who want to see women live long, normal, healthy lives.

That reminds me of something you wrote in your memoir, Promise Me. *You said that your corporate partners' core purpose is profit. If corporate philanthropy and brand-led marketing don't help the companies' bottom lines, should they do it?*

Let me clarify a couple things first. There are several pockets that we get donations from. One is cause-related marketing, where the brands appear with our logo and we get a percentage donated from their purchase price, or a flat donation for a set period. Corporations are also giving larger grants from their corporate foundations, and that's a different pot of money from cause-related marketing.

As for cause-related marketing, if a corporate partner is not doing well, we're not going to do well. We insist on a really balanced relationship. We don't go into one of these programs unless we make sure that the disclosure is correct, our symbols, our messages, and everything else are transparent and clear to the consumer; likewise, partners don't want to go into a program unless they are going to have some visibility with us. I think that's a pretty fair deal, and it returns almost $38 million annually to us in contributions.

What philanthropists inspire you in your work?

One of my favorite donors of all time is David Rubenstein [cofounder of the Carlyle Group, a private equity firm]. He has come to our large affiliate meeting with 1,100 participants. (People come and learn what we're doing, and they take the information back to the affiliates.) David spoke to our grassroots leaders and fund-raisers about philanthropy and how to raise money from people like himself. He is just phenomenal.

Then there are Margaret Hunt Hill and Ruth Altshuler, who were the first major donors to this organization in 1983. Ruth was one of my early mentors. At the time, there weren't that many women mentors. I was lucky enough to find a few women like Ruth. She's unique, inspirational, leads by giving, and gets other people to give. She and Margaret led with their gifts. They led with their knowledge. And they led with their hearts. We need a lot more people like that now, particularly people who want to make a real mark on the work going forward, like David has done.

How will you and your family continue to be involved in SGK?

Well, my son, Eric, is on the board. He grew up with this. He remembers at age five having his room filled with bottles of men's cologne for the first Susan G. Komen fund-raiser in 1983. It was a luncheon in Dallas where [former first lady and breast cancer survivor] Betty Ford was coming to talk, and he remembers that visit because he had a headache for months with all of that stuff in the room. He grew up with more pink than any boy should ever have to! Today, of course, he understands the organization very well. I hope there will always be someone from the family—from Suzy's family—on this board.

And how do you stay fired up?

There is still so much to learn and do. And I wake up every day shocked that I don't know more than I do. There is always something going on that is troublesome, or difficult to handle, or that needs advancing, or that's not going fast enough, or that's going too fast. It's not enough to plan. You have to have that sense of urgency. And the public now is expecting us to do it. We always feel like we're racing. We really are racing for the cure.

"In the United States, virtually everyone has seen the 'pink ribbon' campaigns plastered on everything from makeup and cupcakes to t-shirts and fried chicken buckets, and recognize the symbol as a sign of breast cancer awareness."

I Will Not Be Pinkwashed: Komen's Race Is for Money, Not the Cure

Joseph Mercola

In the following viewpoint, Joseph Mercola accuses the Susan G. Komen organization of engaging in fund-raising practices that line the pockets of well-paid executives instead of the money going toward research to find a breast cancer cure. He says that the Komen foundation's plastering of pink ribbons on thousands of products has more to do with raising awareness of the foundation than it does with curing breast cancer. He reports that the organization partners with companies whose products may con-

tribute to cancer, such as fried chicken and cosmetics that contain cancer-causing ingredients. What is worse, Mercola contends, is that Komen owns stock in several pharmaceutical companies, including AstraZeneca, the maker of a cancer drug that has been found to increase the risk of certain cancers, and in General Electric, a company who makes mammography machinery. Mercola is a doctor of osteopathic medicine and the author of three best-selling books: The Great Bird Flu Hoax, The No-Grain Diet, *and* Effortless Healing.

As you read, consider the following questions:

1. According to the viewpoint, the Komen foundation's assets total how much?

2. What does the term "pinkwashing" describe, according to Mercola?

3. According to the viewpoint, what are some things women can do to prevent breast cancer?

In the United States, virtually everyone has seen the "pink ribbon" campaigns plastered on everything from makeup and cupcakes to t-shirts and fried chicken buckets, and recognize the symbol as a sign of breast cancer awareness.

It's certainly a noble cause, considering that if current trends continue one in 8 U.S. women will be diagnosed with breast cancer at some point during their lives.

Unfortunately, this cause is noble only in appearance; in reality, the multimillion-dollar company behind all those pink ribbons—the Susan G. Komen foundation—uses less than a dime of each dollar to actually look for a breast cancer cure . . . and that's just the surface of the problem. . . .

Former CEO of Komen's "Race for the Cure" Made More than the President of the U.S.

Hala G. Moddelmog, former CEO and president of the Susan G. Komen foundation, made over $550,000 one year—more than President Obama makes (she is now the president of Arby's Restaurant Group).

Employee salaries, or "administrative costs," actually eat up about 11 percent of the company's annual revenues, which might not sound too extreme until you consider what their annual revenues are.

The Komen foundation has assets totaling over $390 million, and according to Charity Navigator had a total revenue of nearly $312 million in the fiscal year ending in March 2010.[i]

A breakdown of how this money was spent was given in a recent article on AlterNet, written by Emily Michele, which showed that only 20.9% of funds are actually used for research—even though a "search for the cure" is their most highly advertised mission.[ii] Where else does the money go?

- 13% for health screening

- 5.6% for treatment

- 10% for fund-raising

- 11.3% for administrative costs

- 39.1% for public education

While public education may seem like a worthwhile effort, this is only true if it includes education about prevention! But as Michele writes:

> "There are no mentions of eating healthy foods, getting proper levels of cancer-preventing Vitamin D, or cutting out sugar—the substance that feeds cancer cells—in any of its 'public health education' efforts. Even though these are scientifically proven ways to prevent cancer."

What it amounts to, more accurately, is a wildly successful advertising campaign, from which the Komen foundation profits handsomely. What is mentioned, often, is the importance of screening for early detection of breast cancer, along with the pink ribbon trademark intended to bring awareness about the disease. Michele continues:

> "It's not curing breast cancer to be aware that you could get it, nor is finding out that you have cancer and treating it in the early stages in hopes of entering into remission. That's not a cure."

Pink Ribbons Are a Money Maker, Not a Cancer Cure

Plastering pink ribbons on every conceivable product has much more to do with raising awareness of the Komen foundation than it does curing breast cancer. As Michele states:

> ". . . the pink-ribbon-plastered 'awareness' and 'education' campaigns are often little more than a highly effective form of advertising—which in turn, brings in Komen's millions. In other words, a way to raise funds for itself, while getting a pat on the back for its efforts to 'save lives.'"

The most atrocious part of this ad campaign is when the ribbons are used on products containing substances that may actually *cause* breast cancer, including:

- Fried chicken

- Yogurt that contains artificial growth hormones linked to breast cancer

- Cosmetics and fragrances that contain cancer-causing chemicals

- Alcohol

The term "pinkwashing" has been coined to describe this deceptive trend, with sponsoring companies claiming they have joined the fight against breast cancer while engaging in practices that contribute to the disease. The Komen foundation receives mega-millions in sponsorship dollars from such corporations.

"Komen receives over $55 million in annual revenue from corporate sponsorships, from such health-minded companies as Coca-Cola, General Mills, and KFC—... Buy a bucket of junk food, and pretend as though you're helping to save lives while you slowly take your own," Michele writes.

Then there are the ties to the drug companies ... it's reported that the Komen foundation owns stock in several pharmaceutical companies, including AstraZeneca, the maker of tamoxifen, a cancer drug that has been found to increase the risk of certain cancers.[iii] They also reportedly own stock in General Electric, which makes mammogram machines. Their focus on early screening, detection and drug treatment fits these ties to a "T," while education about the real underlying causes of cancer are sorely missing from their campaigns.

Komen Founder's First-Class Travel Expenses Also Questioned

The Komen foundation has been making headlines for its recent decision to pull funding to Planned Parenthood (a decision they reversed just days later following public outcry), but less highly publicized is an expense report from Komen founder Nancy Brinker, which was brought forward by the Daily Beast.

Brinker reportedly billed the charity over $133,000 for expenses from June 2007 to January 2009, which might not be so unusual except that at the time she had a full-time job with the federal government, serving as chief of protocol for the State Department. Also questionable are her preferences for five-star hotels and first-class travel, which some former Komen employees have said are "at odds with the organization's important mission."

The Daily Beast reports:[iv]

"... the perception that she could be taking liberties with charity funds could be troublesome, some observers and former colleagues say. [Rick] Cohen of [the journal] *Non-profit Quarterly* points out that first-class travel at a non-profit organization not only is unusual, but also can create the perception that donors' dollars aren't reaching the intended beneficiaries. 'For most nonprofits, they wouldn't think of first-class travel,' he says. 'There is the issue of perception.'"

Perception is reality after all, and it's hard to have a positive perception of a company that *also* reportedly spends nearly $1 million a year suing small charities that use the word "cure" in their names or advertise in pink—even if they're raising money for the same cause! The *Wall Street Journal* reported:[v] "[The Komen foundation is] launching a not-so-friendly legal battle against kite fliers, kayakers and dozens of other themed fund-raisers that it contends are poaching its name. And it's sternly warning charities against dabbling with pink, its signature hue."

American Cancer Society More Interested in Wealth than Health?

The American Cancer Society, which has colored its website with pink ribbons, along with the National Cancer Institute also almost exclusively focus on cancer research and the diagnosis and the chemical treatment of cancer, much like the Komen foundation. The ACS also has close financial ties to both the makers of mammography equipment and cancer drugs, as well as ties to, and financial support from, the pesticide, petrochemical, biotech, cosmetics, and junk food industries—the very industries whose products are the primary contributors to cancer.

Once you realize that these conflicts of interest are there, it becomes quite easy to understand why the ACS and other cancer organizations rarely address the environmental components of cancer, and why information about avoidable toxic exposures are so conspicuously absent from their national "awareness" campaigns. The truth of the matter is that you have to be very careful when donating to any charitable organization, and be sure that the money you are giving is in fact going toward the purpose you intend to support.

In the case of ACS and most other large cancer charities, your money will go toward research to create new, often toxic and sometimes deadly cancer drugs, questionable screening programs like mammography, and into the bank accounts of its numerous well-paid executives—all while the real underlying causes continue to be ignored or intentionally concealed.

What Can You Do to Help Prevent Breast Cancer?

If buying pink t-shirts is not likely to save many lives from breast cancer, what will? I recently interviewed Dr. Christine Horner, a board certified general and plastic surgeon, who shared her extensive knowledge about breast cancer—its causes and treatments, and the pros and cons of various screening methods. I suggest you listen to that interview now, in addition to learning about the many all-natural cancer-prevention strategies below.

- Eat healthy. This means avoid sugar, especially fructose, as all forms of sugar are detrimental to your health in general and promote cancer. Also, focus on eating whole foods and fresh vegetables while avoiding cancer-causing foods.

- Exercise. Research suggests that one of the most powerful ways to lower breast cancer risk substantially is through the simple act of exercise.

- Vitamin D. There's overwhelming evidence pointing to the fact that vitamin D deficiency plays a crucial role in the promotion of cancer. . . . You can decrease your risk of cancer by MORE THAN HALF simply by optimizing your vitamin D levels with adequate sun exposure.

And if you are being treated for cancer it is likely that higher blood levels—probably around 80–90 ng/ml—would be beneficial. The health benefits of optimizing your levels, either by safe sun exposure (ideally), a safe tanning bed, or oral supplementation as a last resort, simply cannot be overstated.

- Get proper sleep, both in terms of getting enough sleep and sleeping between certain optimal hours. According to ayurvedic medicine, the ideal hours for sleep are between 10 p.m. and 6 a.m. Modern research has confirmed the value of this recommendation as certain hormonal fluctuations occur throughout the day and night, and if you engage in the appropriate activities during those times, you're 'riding the wave' so to speak, and are able to get the optimal levels. Working against your biology by staying awake when you should ideally be sleeping or vice versa, interferes with these beneficial hormonal fluctuations.

- Effectively address your stress. The research shows that if you experience a traumatic or highly stressful event, such as a death in the family, your risk of breast cancer is 12 times higher in the ensuing five years. So be sure you tend to your emotional health, not just your physical health.

References

i Charity Navigator, Susan G. Komen for the Cure

ii AlterNet February 4, 2012

iii International Journal of Gynecological Cancer 2007

iv The Daily Beast February 13, 2012

v WSJ.com August 5, 2010

Periodical and Internet Sources Bibliography

The following articles have been selected to supplement the diverse views presented in this chapter.

Julie Beck	"What Good Is 'Raising Awareness?,'" *Atlantic*, April 21, 2015.
Gillian Brockell	"The NFL Is Covered in Pink, but Only a Sliver of Sales Goes to Breast Cancer Research," *Washington Post*, October 16, 2014.
John Brothers	"Breast Cancer Awareness Month Brings the Usual 'Pinkwashing' and Unethical Cause-Marketing Partnerships," *Huffington Post*, October 22, 2014.
Karuna Jaggar	"Komen Is Supposed to Be Curing Breast Cancer. So Why Is Its Pink Ribbon on So Many Carcinogenic Products?," *Washington Post*, October 21, 2014.
Megan Janetsky	"Why Breast Cancer Awareness Is a Marketing Ploy," *State Press* (Tempe, AZ), October 26, 2014.
Amy McCarthy	"Pinkwashing: The Truth Behind Breast Cancer Awareness Products," *Bustle*, October 18, 2013.
Erin Gloria Ryan	"How the NFL's Breast Cancer Awareness Campaign Lies to Women," *Jezebel*, October 1, 2014.
Sandra Steingraber	"Pinkwashing: Fracking Company Teams Up with Susan G. Komen to 'End Breast Cancer Forever,'" *EcoWatch*, October 8, 2014.
Emily Torbett	"Be Cautious When Supporting Breast Cancer Awareness," *Daily Athenaeum* (Morgantown, WV), October 29, 2014.

For Further Discussion

Chapter 1:

1. A study published in the *British Medical Journal (BMJ)* in February 2014 postulated that annual mammography in women aged forty to fifty-nine does not reduce deaths from breast cancer. What are some of the reasons that Robin Hilmantel offers to dispute this claim? Why does Jonathan Cohn state there will never be a conclusive study on the effectiveness of mammograms? Do you agree with their arguments? Explain.

2. Karuna Jaggar is the executive director of Breast Cancer Action. What role do you think her professional background may play in her position on breast cancer screening? Explain your reasoning.

Chapter 2

1. Several authors in this chapter write about the impact Angelina Jolie's decision to have a prophylactic mastectomy has had on women seeking out genetic counseling. Why do you believe Jolie's announcement of her procedure has had such a profound impact? Explain your reasoning.

2. Lisa Newman and the experts at the Dana-Farber Cancer Institute write that there is no evidence that having a double mastectomy benefits women with early-stage breast cancer in one breast. What do you believe are some of the reasons that women might opt for a double mastectomy, despite this evidence?

3. Colleen Joy McCullough writes that women of color are less likely than white women to seek genetic counseling for breast cancer. Why do you believe this is the case? Explain.

Chapter 3

1. Abby Ohlheiser disputes the findings of a study by Yubei Huang and colleagues that found that abortion is linked to breast cancer based on their study of Chinese women. Ohlheiser finds fault with the study because it was primarily based on self-reported results, and she claims women with breast cancer are more likely to be truthful about their reproductive histories than the general population. Do you agree with Ohlheiser? Do you think self-reporting could impact the results of a study? Explain.

2. Joel Brind and Mary L. Davenport claim that pro-choice advocates are attacking the Chinese study linking abortion to breast cancer to further their political agenda. Joyce Arthur argues that pro-life advocates are promoting the study to further their political agenda. Whose position do you agree with, and why? Explain.

Chapter 4

1. Lea Goldman argues that too much money goes to breast cancer awareness and too little funds go to research to find a cure. She suggests individuals should avoid pink ribbon merchandise and instead should donate to cancer organizations that spend most of their funds on research and treatment. Do you think that is sound advice? Explain.

2. Nancy Brinker speaks of the positive impact the Susan G. Komen organization has had in finding a cure for breast cancer. Joseph Mercola accuses the Komen organization of raising funds to further its own agenda rather than using the money to find a breast cancer cure. Brinker's background is in marketing; Mercola is a doctor of osteopathic medicine. What is there in Brinker's and Mercola's backgrounds that might lead them to different perspectives on the Komen foundation? What is your opinion of the Komen foundation? Explain your reasoning.

Organizations to Contact

The editors have compiled the following list of organizations concerned with the issues debated in this book. The descriptions are derived from materials provided by the organizations. All have publications or information available for interested readers. The list was compiled on the date of publication of the present volume; the information provided here may change. Be aware that many organizations take several weeks or longer to respond to inquiries, so allow as much time as possible.

American Breast Cancer Foundation (ABCF)
10400 Little Patuxent Parkway, Suite 480
Columbia, MD   21044
(410) 730-5105
e-mail: info@abcf.org
website: www.abcf.org

The mission of the American Breast Cancer Foundation (ABCF) is to provide financial assistance for breast cancer screenings and diagnostic tests for uninsured and underinsured individuals. Among the programs of the ABCF is Fit for Life, which is designed to provide education on the role of regular physical activity and proper diet in the prevention and treatment of breast cancer. The ABCF website offers news, testimonials, and a blog.

American Cancer Society (ACS)
250 Williams Street NW, Atlanta, GA   30303-1002
(800) 227-2345
website: www.cancer.org

Founded in 1913, the American Cancer Society (ACS) serves as a nationwide, community-based, voluntary health organization dedicated to eliminating cancer through prevention, treatment, research, education, advocacy, and service. Among the services offered by ACS is the Reach to Recovery program, where in breast cancer survivors provide counseling to those coping with breast cancer. Among the organization's publications is *Breast Cancer Journey: The Essential Guide to Treatment and Recovery.* The ACS website has a page dedicated to breast cancer that provides detailed information, including statistics, testimonials, studies, and news on the latest developments in the disease.

Breast Cancer Action

657 Mission Street, Suite 302, San Francisco, CA   94105
(415) 243-9301 • fax: (415) 243-3996
e-mail: info@bcaction.org
website: www.bcaction.org

The mission of Breast Cancer Action is to focus on systemic interventions that will address the root causes of breast cancer and produce broad public health benefits. The organization contrasts itself from the mainstream breast cancer movement, which it believes is mistakenly focused on pink ribbons, awareness campaigns, and mammography screening. The website of Breast Cancer Action provides education resources such as webinars, fact sheets, and tool kits, as well as a blog with entries such as "New Study Shows Half of Women with Dense Breasts Have Average to Low Cancer Risk."

Breast Cancer Alliance

48 Maple Avenue, Greenwich, CT   06830
(203) 861-0014
e-mail: info@breastcanceralliance.org
website: www.breastcanceralliance.org

The mission of the Breast Cancer Alliance is to improve survival rates and quality of life for those impacted by breast cancer through better prevention, early detection, treatment, and cure. To further these goals, the organization invests in research, breast surgery fellowships, regional education, and support and screening for the uninsured and underinsured. Its website provides archives of its *Outlook* newsletter and answers to frequently asked questions regarding breast cancer.

Breastcancer.org

120 East Lancaster Avenue, Suite 201, Ardmore, PA 19003
(610) 642-6550
website: www.breastcancer.org

The mission of Breastcancer.org is to help breast cancer patients and their families understand the complex medical and personal information about breast cancer so they can make the best decisions for their treatment. The Breastcancer.org website includes breast cancer information including symptoms and diagnosis, treatment and side effects, and day-to-day matters. Among the organization's publications are "Your Guide to the Breast Cancer Pathology Report" and "Think Pink, Live Green: A Step-by-Step Guide to Reducing Your Risk of Breast Cancer."

Breast Cancer Research Foundation (BCRF)

60 East Fifty-Sixth Street, 8th Floor, New York, NY 10022
(646) 497-2600
e-mail: bcrf@bcrfcure.org
website: www.bcrfcure.org

The Breast Cancer Research Foundation (BCRF) is a nonprofit organization committed to achieving prevention and a cure for breast cancer. The organization provides funding for cancer research worldwide to promote advances in tumor biology, genetics, prevention, treatment, metastasis, and survivorship. In 2015, BCRF stated it would award $47 million in annual grants to 226 scientists studying breast cancer around the world. The organization's website includes news items and *The Progress Report* blog, with entries such as "New Device Brings Us Closer to Understanding Metastasis, the Most Fatal Element of Cancer."

Dr. Susan Love Research Foundation

2811 Wilshire Boulevard, Suite 500, Santa Monica, CA 90403
(310) 828-0060 • fax: (310) 828-5403
website: www.dslrf.org

The mission of the Dr. Susan Love Research Foundation is to achieve a future without breast cancer by engaging the public and scientific communities in research on cause and prevention. The foundation focuses its research on the breast ducts and in understanding how breasts function. The foundation's website includes news items and links to support groups and advocacy organizations, as well as a blog with entries such as "Sometimes, Diagnosis Is in the Eye of the Beholder" and "Research Worth Watching: Digging into Metastatic Disease."

National Breast Cancer Coalition (NBCC)
1010 Vermont Avenue NW, Suite 900, Washington, DC   20005
(800) 622-2838 • fax: (202) 265-6854
website: www.breastcancerdeadline2020.org

In 2010, the National Breast Cancer Coalition (NBCC) launched Breast Cancer Deadline 2020—challenging policy makers, researchers, breast cancer advocates, and other stakeholders to know how to end the disease by 2020. The goals of NBCC are to promote research, improve access to quality breast cancer care for all women, and educate and empower men and women as advocates. NBCC also lobbies Congress for improved public policies regarding breast cancer. The NBCC website offers fact sheets, position papers, and progress reports on the state of breast cancer.

National Breast Cancer Foundation (NBCF)
2600 Network Boulevard, Suite 300, Frisco, TX   75034
website: www.nationalbreastcancer.org

The mission of the National Breast Cancer Foundation (NBCF) is to provide help and hope to those affected by breast cancer through early detection, education, and support services. Among the programs that NBCF offers are the National Mammography Program, Beyond the Shock, Early Detection Plan, and Breast Health Education. The website includes information on breast cancer, descriptions of NBCF programs, and press releases, as well as the *NBCF Blog* with entries such as "Surviving and Thriving Through Hope" and "Look Ahead and Prepare."

National Cancer Institute (NCI)

BG 9609 MSC 9760, Bethesda, MD   20892-9760
(800) 422-6237
website: www.cancer.gov

Part of the National Institutes of Health of the US Department of Health and Human Services, the National Cancer Institute (NCI) provides resources to individual researchers and institutions, conducts cancer research, and provides leadership to national infrastructures that care for patients and develop new methods to treat and prevent cancer. The NCI website includes information on the treatment, prevention and causes, screening and testing, clinical trials, and research conducted on breast cancer.

Susan G. Komen

5005 LBJ Freeway, Suite 250, Dallas, TX   75244
(877) 465-6636
website: ww5.komen.org

The Susan G. Komen organization is the world's largest non-profit source of funding for the fight against breast cancer. The organization addresses breast cancer on multiple fronts, including research, community health, global outreach, and public policy initiatives. One of the organization's premier fund-raising events is Race for the Cure, a series of five-kilometer runs and fitness walks that raise funds for and awareness of breast cancer. The organization's website provides information about breast cancer, including facts and statistics, risk factors, screening and detection, diagnosis, treatment, and quality of life topics. Additionally, the Komen website offers news, press releases, videos, fact sheets, discussion guides, tool kits, and other learning materials.

Bibliography of Books

Greg Anderson *Breast Cancer: 50 Essential Things to Do.* San Francisco, CA: Conari Press, 2011.

Robert A. Aronowitz *Unnatural History: Breast Cancer and American Society.* New York: Cambridge University Press, 2007.

George R. Blumenschein *Quest for the Cure: Reflections on the Evolution of Breast Cancer Treatment.* Waltham, MA: Academic Press, 2013.

Nancy G. Brinker *Promise Me: How a Sister's Love Launched the Global Movement to End Breast Cancer.* New York: Three Rivers Press, 2010.

Grace Budrys *Unequal Health: How Inequality Contributes to Health or Illness.* Lanham, MD: Rowman & Littlefield Publishers, 2010.

Barbara Delinsky *Uplift: Secrets from the Sisterhood of Breast Cancer Survivors.* New York: Atria Books, 2011.

Jackie Fox *From Zero to Mastectomy: What I Learned and You Need to Know About Stage 0 Breast Cancer.* Gretna, NE: Honyocker Press, 2010.

Sue Friedman, Rebecca Sutphen, and Kathy Steligo *Confronting Hereditary Breast and Ovarian Cancer: Identify Your Risk, Understand Your Options, Change Your Destiny.* Baltimore, MD: Johns Hopkins University Press, 2012.

Peter C. Gotzsche *Mammography Screening: Truth, Lies and Controversy.* London: Radcliffe Publishing Ltd., 2012.

Karen Handel *Planned Bullyhood: The Truth Behind the Headlines About the Planned Parenthood Funding Battle with the Susan G. Komen for the Cure.* Brentwood, TN: Howard Books, 2012.

Hollye Jacobs and Elizabeth Messina *The Silver Lining: A Supportive and Insightful Guide to Breast Cancer.* New York: Atria Books, 2014.

Frances G. Joyce *Dancing in the Rain: Surviving Breast Cancer and Learning to Embrace Life.* Seattle, WA: CreateSpace, 2011.

Samantha King *Pink Ribbons, Inc.: Breast Cancer and the Politics of Philanthropy.* Minneapolis: University of Minnesota Press, 2008.

Maren Klawiter *The Biopolitics of Breast Cancer: Changing Cultures of Disease and Activism.* Minneapolis: University of Minnesota Press, 2008.

Philip Kotler, David Hessekiel, and Nancy Lee *Good Works!: Marketing and Corporate Initiatives That Build a Better World ... and the Bottom Line.* Hoboken, NJ: John Wiley & Sons, 2012.

John Link — *The Breast Cancer Survival Manual: A Step-by-Step Guide for Women with Newly Diagnosed Breast Cancer.* 5th ed. New York: Henry Holt, 2012.

Susan M. Love — *Dr. Susan Love's Breast Book.* 5th ed. Philadelphia, PA: Da Capo Books, 2015.

Paul Marks and James Sterngold — *On the Cancer Frontier: One Man, One Disease, and a Medical Revolution.* Philadelphia, PA: PublicAffairs, 2014.

Mayo Clinic — *The Mayo Clinic Breast Cancer Book.* Philadelphia, PA: Da Capo Books, 2012.

Sabrina McCormick — *No Family History: The Environmental Links to Breast Cancer.* Lanham, MD: Rowman & Littlefield Publishers, 2009.

Sarah E.H. Moore — *Ribbon Culture: Charity, Compassion, and Public Awareness.* New York: Palgrave Macmillan, 2008.

Andrea Farkas Patenaude — *Prophylactic Mastectomy: Insights from Women Who Chose to Reduce Their Risk.* Santa Barbara, CA: Praeger, 2012.

Handel Reynolds — *The Big Squeeze: A Social and Political History of the Controversial Mammogram.* Ithaca, NY: Cornell University Press, 2012.

Mahesh K. Shetty, ed. *Breast Cancer Screening and Diagnosis: A Synopsis.* New York: Springer, 2014.

Madhulika Sikka *A Breast Cancer Alphabet.* New York: Crown, 2014.

Gayle A. Sulik *Pink Ribbon Blues: How Breast Cancer Culture Undermines Women's Health.* New York: Oxford University Press, 2011.

Michael H. Torosian, ed. *Breast Cancer: A Guide to Detection and Multidisciplinary Therapy.* Totowa, NJ: Humana Press, 2010.

H. Gilbert Welch, Lisa Schwartz, and Steve Woloshin *Overdiagnosed: Making People Sick in the Pursuit of Health.* Boston, MA: Beacon Press, 2011.

Index